The Poetry of Algernon Charles Swinburne

VOLUME III – SONGS BEFORE SUNRISE

Algernon Charles Swinburne was born on April 5th, 1837, in London, into a wealthy Northumbrian family. He was educated at Eton and at Balliol College, Oxford, but did not complete a degree.

In 1860 Swinburne published two verse dramas but achieved his first literary success in 1865 with Atalanta in Calydon, written in the form of classical Greek tragedy. The following year "Poems and Ballads" brought him instant notoriety. He was now identified with "indecent" themes and the precept of art for art's sake.

Although he produced much after this success in general his popularity and critical reputation declined. The most important qualities of Swinburne's work are an intense lyricism, his intricately extended and evocative imagery, metrical virtuosity, rich use of assonance and alliteration, and bold, complex rhythms.

Swinburne's physical appearance was small, frail, and plagued by several other oddities of physique and temperament. Throughout the 1860s and 1870s he drank excessively and was prone to accidents that often left him bruised, bloody, or unconscious. Until his forties he suffered intermittent physical collapses that necessitated removal to his parents' home while he recovered.

Throughout his career Swinburne also published literary criticism of great worth. His deep knowledge of world literatures contributed to a critical style rich in quotation, allusion, and comparison. He is particularly noted for discerning studies of Elizabethan dramatists and of many English and French poets and novelists. As well he was a noted essayist and wrote two novels.

In 1879, Swinburne's friend and literary agent, Theodore Watts-Dunton, intervened during a time when Swinburne was dangerously ill. Watts-Dunton isolated Swinburne at a suburban home in Putney and gradually weaned him from alcohol, former companions and many other habits as well.

Much of his poetry in this period may be inferior but some individual poems are exceptional; "By the North Sea," "Evening on the Broads," "A Nympholept," "The Lake of Gaube," and "Neap-Tide."

Swinburne lived another thirty years with Watts-Dunton. He denied Swinburne's friends access to him, controlled the poet's money, and restricted his activities. It is often quoted that 'he saved the man but killed the poet'.

Swinburne died on April 10th, 1909 at the age of seventy-two.

Index of Content

Dedication to Joseph Mazzini

Take, since you bade it should bear,
These, of the seed of your sowing,
Blossom or berry or weed.
Sweet though they be not, or fair,
That the dew of your word kept growing,
Sweet at least was the seed.

Men bring you love-offerings of tears,
And sorrow the kiss that assuages,
And slaves the hate-offering of wrongs,
And time the thanksgiving of years,
And years the thanksgiving of ages;
I bring you my handful of songs.

If a perfume be left, if a bloom,
Let it live till Italia be risen,
To be strewn in the dust of her car
When her voice shall awake from the tomb
England, and France from her prison,
Sisters, a star by a star.

I bring you the sword of a song,
The sword of my spirit's desire,
Feeble; but laid at your feet,
That which was weak shall be strong,
That which was cold shall take fire,
That which was bitter be sweet.

It was wrought not with hands to smite,
Nor hewn after swordsmiths' fashion,
Nor tempered on anvil of steel;
But with visions and dreams of the night,
But with hope, and the patience of passion,
And the signet of love for a seal.

Be it witness, till one more strong,
Till a loftier lyre, till a rarer
Lute praise her better than I,
Be it witness before you, my song,
That I knew her, the world's banner-bearer,
Who shall cry the republican cry.

Yea, even she as at first,
Yea, she alone and none other,
Shall cast down, shall build up, shall bring home;
Slake earth's hunger and thirst,
Lighten, and lead as a mother;
First name of the world's names, Rome.

PRELUDE

Between the green bud and the red
Youth sat and sang by Time, and shed

From eyes and tresses flowers and tears,
From heart and spirit hopes and fears,
Upon the hollow stream whose bed
Is channelled by the foamless years;
And with the white the gold-haired head
Mixed running locks, and in Time's ears
Youth's dreams hung singing, and Time's truth
Was half not harsh in the ears of Youth.
Between the bud and the blown flower
Youth talked with joy and grief an hour,
With footless joy and wingless grief
And twin-born faith and disbelief
Who share the seasons to devour;
And long ere these made up their sheaf
Felt the winds round him shake and shower
The rose-red and the blood-red leaf,
Delight whose germ grew never grain,
And passion dyed in its own pain.

Then he stood up, and trod to dust
Fear and desire, mistrust and trust,
And dreams of bitter sleep and sweet,
And bound for sandals on his feet
Knowledge and patience of what must
And what things may be, in the heat
And cold of years that rot and rust
And alter; and his spirit's meat
Was freedom, and his staff was wrought
Of strength, and his cloak woven of thought.

For what has he whose will sees clear
To do with doubt and faith and fear,
Swift hopes and slow despondencies?
His heart is equal with the sea's
And with the sea-wind's, and his ear
Is level to the speech of these,
And his soul communes and takes cheer
With the actual earth's equalities,
Air, light, and night, hills, winds, and streams,
And seeks not strength from strengthless dreams.

His soul is even with the sun
Whose spirit and whose eye are one,
Who seeks not stars by day, nor light
And heavy heat of day by night.
Him can no God cast down, whom none
Can lift in hope beyond the height
Of fate and nature and things done

By the calm rule of might and right
That bids men be and bear and do,
And die beneath blind skies or blue.

To him the lights of even and morn
Speak no vain things of love or scorn,
Fancies and passions miscreate
By man in things dispassionate.
Nor holds he fellowship forlorn
With souls that pray and hope and hate,
And doubt they had better not been born,
And fain would lure or scare off fate
And charm their doomsman from their doom
And make fear dig its own false tomb.

He builds not half of doubts and half
Of dreams his own soul's cenotaph,
Whence hopes and fears with helpless eyes,
Wrapt loose in cast-off cerecloths, rise
And dance and wring their hands and laugh,
And weep thin tears and sigh light sighs,
And without living lips would quaff
The living spring in man that lies,
And drain his soul of faith and strength
It might have lived on a life's length.

He hath given himself and hath not sold
To God for heaven or man for gold,
Or grief for comfort that it gives,
Or joy for grief's restoratives.
He hath given himself to time, whose fold
Shuts in the mortal flock that lives
On its plain pasture's heat and cold
And the equal year's alternatives.
Earth, heaven, and time, death, life, and he,
Endure while they shall be to be.

"Yet between death and life are hours
To flush with love and hide in flowers;
What profit save in these?" men cry:
"Ah, see, between soft earth and sky,
What only good things here are ours!"
They say, "what better wouldst thou try,
What sweeter sing of? or what powers
Serve, that will give thee ere thou die
More joy to sing and be less sad,
More heart to play and grow more glad?"

Play then and sing; we too have played,
We likewise, in that subtle shade.
We too have twisted through our hair
Such tendrils as the wild Loves wear,
And heard what mirth the Maenads made,
Till the wind blew our garlands bare
And left their roses disarrayed,
And smote the summer with strange air,
And disengirdled and discrowned
The limbs and locks that vine-wreaths bound.

We too have tracked by star-proof trees
The tempest of the Thyiades
Scare the loud night on hills that hid
The blood-feasts of the Bassarid,
Heard their song's iron cadences
Fright the wolf hungering from the kid,
Outroar the lion-throated seas,
Outchide the north-wind if it chid,
And hush the torrent-tongued ravines
With thunders of their tambourines.

But the fierce flute whose notes acclaim
Dim goddesses of fiery fame,
Cymbal and clamorous kettledrum,
Timbrels and tabrets, all are dumb
That turned the high chill air to flame;
The singing tongues of fire are numb
That called on Cotys by her name
Edonian, till they felt her come
And maddened, and her mystic face
Lightened along the streams of Thrace.

For Pleasure slumberless and pale,
And Passion with rejected veil,
Pass, and the tempest-footed throng
Of hours that follow them with song
Till their feet flag and voices fail,
And lips that were so loud so long
Learn silence, or a wearier wail;
So keen is change, and time so strong,
To weave the robes of life and rend
And weave again till life have end.

But weak is change, but strengthless time,
To take the light from heaven, or climb
The hills of heaven with wasting feet.
Songs they can stop that earth found meet,

But the stars keep their ageless rhyme;
Flowers they can slay that spring thought sweet,
But the stars keep their spring sublime;
Passions and pleasures can defeat,
Actions and agonies control,
And life and death, but not the soul.

Because man's soul is man's God still,
What wind soever waft his will
Across the waves of day and night
To port or shipwreck, left or right,
By shores and shoals of good and ill;
And still its flame at mainmast height
Through the rent air that foam-flakes fill
Sustains the indomitable light
Whence only man hath strength to steer
Or helm to handle without fear.

Save his own soul's light overhead,
None leads him, and none ever led,
Across birth's hidden harbour-bar,
Past youth where shoreward shallows are,
Through age that drives on toward the red
Vast void of sunset hailed from far,
To the equal waters of the dead;
Save his own soul he hath no star,
And sinks, except his own soul guide,
Helmless in middle turn of tide.

No blast of air or fire of sun
Puts out the light whereby we run
With girded loins our lamplit race,
And each from each takes heart of grace
And spirit till his turn be done,
And light of face from each man's face
In whom the light of trust is one;
Since only souls that keep their place
By their own light, and watch things roll,
And stand, have light for any soul.

A little time we gain from time
To set our seasons in some chime,
For harsh or sweet or loud or low,
With seasons played out long ago
And souls that in their time and prime
Took part with summer or with snow,
Lived abject lives out or sublime,
And had their chance of seed to sow

For service or disservice done
To those days dead and this their son.

A little time that we may fill
Or with such good works or such ill
As loose the bonds or make them strong
Wherein all manhood suffers wrong.
By rose-hung river and light-foot rill
There are who rest not; who think long
Till they discern as from a hill
At the sun's hour of morning song,
Known of souls only, and those souls free,
The sacred spaces of the sea.

THE EVE OF REVOLUTION

I

The trumpets of the four winds of the world
From the ends of the earth blow battle; the night heaves,
With breasts palpitating and wings refurled,
With passion of couched limbs, as one who grieves
Sleeping, and in her sleep she sees uncurled
Dreams serpent-shapen, such as sickness weaves,
Down the wild wind of vision caught and whirled,
Dead leaves of sleep, thicker than autumn leaves,
Shadows of storm-shaped things,
Flights of dim tribes of kings,
The reaping men that reap men for their sheaves,
And, without grain to yield,
Their scythe-swept harvest-field
Thronged thick with men pursuing and fugitives,
Dead foliage of the tree of sleep,
Leaves blood-coloured and golden, blown from deep to deep.

II

I hear the midnight on the mountains cry
With many tongues of thunders, and I hear
Sound and resound the hollow shield of sky
With trumpet-throated winds that charge and cheer,
And through the roar of the hours that fighting fly,
Through flight and fight and all the fluctuant fear,
A sound sublimer than the heavens are high,
A voice more instant than the winds are clear,

Say to my spirit, "Take
Thy trumpet too, and make
A rallying music in the void night's ear,
Till the storm lose its track,
And all the night go back;
Till, as through sleep false life knows true life near,
Thou know the morning through the night,
And through the thunder silence, and through darkness light."

III

I set the trumpet to my lips and blow.
The height of night is shaken, the skies break,
The winds and stars and waters come and go
By fits of breath and light and sound, that wake
As out of sleep, and perish as the show
Built up of sleep, when all her strengths forsake
The sense-compelling spirit; the depths glow,
The heights flash, and the roots and summits shake
Of earth in all her mountains,
And the inner foamless fountains
And wellsprings of her fast-bound forces quake;
Yea, the whole air of life
Is set on fire of strife,
Till change unmake things made and love remake;
Reason and love, whose names are one,
Seeing reason is the sunlight shed from love the sun.

IV

The night is broken eastward; is it day,
Or but the watchfires trembling here and there,
Like hopes on memory's devastated way,
In moonless wastes of planet-stricken air?
O many-childed mother great and grey,
O multitudinous bosom, and breasts that bare
Our fathers' generations, whereat lay
The weanling peoples and the tribes that were,
Whose new-born mouths long dead
Those ninefold nipples fed,
Dim face with deathless eyes and withered hair,
Fostress of obscure lands,
Whose multiplying hands
Wove the world's web with divers races fair
And cast it waif-wise on the stream,
The waters of the centuries, where thou sat'st to dream;

V

O many-minded mother and visionary,
Asia, that sawest their westering waters sweep
With all the ships and spoils of time to carry
And all the fears and hopes of life to keep,
Thy vesture wrought of ages legendary
Hides usward thine impenetrable sleep,
And thy veiled head, night's oldest tributary,
We know not if it speak or smile or weep.
But where for us began
The first live light of man
And first-born fire of deeds to burn and leap,
The first war fair as peace
To shine and lighten Greece,
And the first freedom moved upon the deep,
God's breath upon the face of time
Moving, a present spirit, seen of men sublime;

VI

There where our east looks always to thy west,
Our mornings to thine evenings, Greece to thee,
These lights that catch the mountains crest by crest,
Are they of stars or beacons that we see?
Taygetus takes here the winds abreast,
And there the sun resumes Thermopylae;
The light is Athens where those remnants rest,
And Salamis the sea-wall of that sea.
The grass men tread upon
Is very Marathon,
The leaves are of that time-unstricken tree
That storm nor sun can fret
Nor wind, since she that set
Made it her sign to men whose shield was she;
Here, as dead time his deathless things,
Eurotas and Cephisus keep their sleepless springs.

VII

O hills of Crete, are these things dead? O waves,
O many-mouthed streams, are these springs dry?
Earth, dost thou feed and hide now none but slaves?
Heaven, hast thou heard of men that would not die?

Is the land thick with only such men's graves
As were ashamed to look upon the sky?
Ye dead, whose name outfaces and outbraves
Death, is the seed of such as you gone by?
Sea, have thy ports not heard
Some Marathonian word
Rise up to landward and to Godward fly?
No thunder, that the skies
Sent not upon us, rise
With fire and earthquake and a cleaving cry?
Nay, light is here, and shall be light,
Though all the face of the hour be overborne with night.

VIII

I set the trumpet to my lips and blow.
The night is broken northward; the pale plains
And footless fields of sun-forgotten snow
Feel through their creviced lips and iron veins
Such quick breath labour and such clean blood flow
As summer-stricken spring feels in her pains
When dying May bears June, too young to know
The fruit that waxes from the flower that wanes;
Strange tyrannies and vast,
Tribes frost-bound to their past,
Lands that are loud all through their length with chains,
Wastes where the wind's wings break,
Displumed by daylong ache
And anguish of blind snows and rack-blown rains,
And ice that seals the White Sea's lips,
Whose monstrous weights crush flat the sides of shrieking ships;

IX

Horrible sights and sounds of the unreached pole,
And shrill fierce climes of inconsolable air,
Shining below the beamless aureole
That hangs about the north-wind's hurtling hair,
A comet-lighted lamp, sublime and sole
Dawn of the dayless heaven where suns despair;
Earth, skies, and waters, smitten into soul,
Feel the hard veil that iron centuries wear
Rent as with hands in sunder,
Such hands as make the thunder
And clothe with form all substance and strip bare;
Shapes, shadows, sounds and lights

Of their dead days and nights
Take soul of life too keen for death to bear;
Life, conscience, forethought, will, desire,
Flood men's inanimate eyes and dry-drawn hearts with fire.

X

Light, light, and light! to break and melt in sunder
All clouds and chains that in one bondage bind
Eyes, hands, and spirits, forged by fear and wonder
And sleek fierce fraud with hidden knife behind;
There goes no fire from heaven before their thunder,
Nor are the links not malleable that wind
Round the snared limbs and souls that ache thereunder;
The hands are mighty, were the head not blind.
Priest is the staff of king,
And chains and clouds one thing,
And fettered flesh with devastated mind.
Open thy soul to see,
Slave, and thy feet are free;
Thy bonds and thy beliefs are one in kind,
And of thy fears thine irons wrought
Hang weights upon thee fashioned out of thine own thought.

XI

O soul, O God, O glory of liberty,
To night and day their lightning and their light!
With heat of heart thou kindlest the quick sea,
And the dead earth takes spirit from thy sight;
The natural body of things is warm with thee,
And the world's weakness parcel of thy might;
Thou seest us feeble and forceless, fit to be
Slaves of the years that drive us left and right,
Drowned under hours like waves
Wherethrough we row like slaves;
But if thy finger touch us, these take flight.
If but one sovereign word
Of thy live lips be heard,
What man shall stop us, and what God shall smite?
Do thou but look in our dead eyes,
They are stars that light each other till thy sundawn rise.

XII

Thou art the eye of this blind body of man,
The tongue of this dumb people; shalt thou not
See, shalt thou speak not for them?
Time is wan And hope is weak with waiting, and swift thought
Hath lost the wings at heel wherewith he ran,
And on the red pit's edge sits down distraught
To talk with death of days republican
And dreams and fights long since dreamt out and fought;
Of the last hope that drew
To that red edge anew
The firewhite faith of Poland without spot;
Of the blind Russian might,
And fire that is not light;
Of the green Rhineland where thy spirit wrought;
But though time, hope, and memory tire,
Canst thou wax dark as they do, thou whose light is fire?

XIII

I set the trumpet to my lips and blow.
The night is broken westward; the wide sea
That makes immortal motion to and fro
From world's end unto world's end, and shall be
When nought now grafted of men's hands shall grow
And as the weed in last year's waves are we
Or spray the sea-wind shook a year ago
From its sharp tresses down the storm to lee,
The moving god that hides
Time in its timeless tides
Wherein time dead seems live eternity,
That breaks and makes again
Much mightier things than men,
Doth it not hear change coming, or not see?
Are the deeps deaf and dead and blind,
To catch no light or sound from landward of mankind?

XIV

O thou, clothed round with raiment of white waves,
Thy brave brows lightening through the grey wet air,
Thou, lulled with sea-sounds of a thousand caves,
And lit with sea-shine to thine inland lair,
Whose freedom clothed the naked souls of slaves
And stripped the muffled souls of tyrants bare,
O, by the centuries of thy glorious graves,
By the live light of the earth that was thy care,

Live, thou must not be dead,
Live; let thine armed head
Lift itself up to sunward and the fair
Daylight of time and man,
Thine head republican,
With the same splendour on thine helmless hair
That in his eyes kept up a light
Who on thy glory gazed away their sacred sight;

XV

Who loved and looked their sense to death on thee;
Who taught thy lips imperishable things,
And in thine ears outsang thy singing sea;
Who made thy foot firm on the necks of kings
And thy soul somewhile steadfast—woe are we
It was but for a while, and all the strings
Were broken of thy spirit; yet had he
Set to such tunes and clothed it with such wings
It seemed for his sole sake
Impossible to break,
And woundless of the worm that waits and stings,
The golden-headed worm
Made headless for a term,
The king-snake whose life kindles with the spring's,
To breathe his soul upon her bloom,
And while she marks not turn her temple to her tomb.

XVI

By those eyes blinded and that heavenly head
And the secluded soul adorable,
O Milton's land, what ails thee to be dead?
Thine ears are yet sonorous with his shell
That all the songs of all thy sea-line fed
With motive sound of spring-tides at mid swell,
And through thine heart his thought as blood is shed,
Requickening thee with wisdom to do well;
Such sons were of thy womb,
England, for love of whom
Thy name is not yet writ with theirs that fell,
But, till thou quite forget
What were thy children, yet
On the pale lips of hope is as a spell;
And Shelley's heart and Landor's mind
Lit thee with latter watch-fires; why wilt thou be blind?

Though all were else indifferent, all that live
Spiritless shapes of nations; though time wait
In vain on hope till these have help to give,
And faith and love crawl famished from the gate;
Canst thou sit shamed and self-contemplative
With soulless eyes on thy secluded fate?
Though time forgive them, thee shall he forgive,
Whose choice was in thine hand to be so great?
Who cast out of thy mind
The passion of man's kind,
And made thee and thine old name separate?
Now when time looks to see
New names and old and thee
Build up our one Republic state by state,
England with France, and France with Spain,
And Spain with sovereign Italy strike hands and reign.

O known and unknown fountain-heads that fill
Our dear life-springs of England! O bright race
Of streams and waters that bear witness still
To the earth her sons were made of! O fair face
Of England, watched of eyes death cannot kill,
How should the soul that lit you for a space
Fall through sick weakness of a broken will
To the dead cold damnation of disgrace?
Such wind of memory stirs
On all green hills of hers,
Such breath of record from so high a place,
From years whose tongues of flame
Prophesied in her name
Her feet should keep truth's bright and burning trace,
We needs must have her heart with us,
Whose hearts are one with man's; she must be dead or thus.

Who is against us? who is on our side?
Whose heart of all men's hearts is one with man's?
Where art thou that wast prophetess and bride,
When truth and thou trod under time and chance?

What latter light of what new hope shall guide
Out of the snares of hell thy feet, O France?
What heel shall bruise these heads that hiss and glide,
What wind blow out these fen-born fires that dance
Before thee to thy death?
No light, no life, no breath,
From thy dead eyes and lips shall take the trance,
Till on that deadliest crime
Reddening the feet of time
Who treads through blood and passes, time shall glance
Pardon, and Italy forgive,
And Rome arise up whom thou slewest, and bid thee live.

XX

I set the trumpet to my lips and blow.
The night is broken southward; the springs run,
The daysprings and the watersprings that flow
Forth with one will from where their source was one,
Out of the might of morning: high and low,
The hungering hills feed full upon the sun,
The thirsting valleys drink of him and glow
As a heart burns with some divine thing done,
Or as blood burns again
In the bruised heart of Spain,
A rose renewed with red new life begun,
Dragged down with thorns and briers,
That puts forth buds like fires
Till the whole tree take flower in unison,
And prince that clogs and priest that clings
Be cast as weeds upon the dunghill of dead things.

XXI

Ah heaven, bow down, be nearer! This is she,
Italia, the world's wonder, the world's care,
Free in her heart ere quite her hands be free,
And lovelier than her loveliest robe of air.
The earth hath voice, and speech is in the sea,
Sounds of great joy, too beautiful to bear;
All things are glad because of her, but we
Most glad, who loved her when the worst days were.
O sweetest, fairest, first,
O flower, when times were worst,
Thou hadst no stripe wherein we had no share.
Have not our hearts held close,

Kept fast the whole world's rose?
Have we not worn thee at heart whom none would wear?
First love and last love, light of lands,
Shall we not touch thee full-blown with our lips and hands?

XXII

O too much loved, what shall we say of thee?
What shall we make of our heart's burning fire,
The passion in our lives that fain would be
Made each a brand to pile into the pyre
That shall burn up thy foemen, and set free
The flame whence thy sun-shadowing wings aspire?
Love of our life, what more than men are we,
That this our breath for thy sake should expire,
For whom to joyous death
Glad gods might yield their breath,
Great gods drop down from heaven to serve for hire?
We are but men, are we,
And thou art Italy;
What shall we do for thee with our desire?
What gift shall we deserve to give?
How shall we die to do thee service, or how live?

XXIII

The very thought in us how much we love thee
Makes the throat sob with love and blinds the eyes.
How should love bear thee, to behold above thee
His own light burning from reverberate skies?
They give thee light, but the light given them of thee
Makes faint the wheeling fires that fall and rise.
What love, what life, what death of man's should move thee,
What face that lingers or what foot that flies?
It is not heaven that lights
Thee with such days and nights,
But thou that heaven is lit from in such wise.
O thou her dearest birth,
Turn thee to lighten earth,
Earth too that bore thee and yearns to thee and cries;
Stand up, shine, lighten, become flame,
Till as the sun's name through all nations be thy name.

XXIV

I take the trumpet from my lips and sing.
O life immeasurable and imminent love,
And fear like winter leading hope like spring,
Whose flower-bright brows the day-star sits above,
Whose hand unweariable and untiring wing
Strike music from a world that wailed and strove,
Each bright soul born and every glorious thing,
From very freedom to man's joy thereof,
O time, O change and death,
Whose now not hateful breath
But gives the music swifter feet to move
Through sharp remeasuring tones
Of refluent antiphones
More tender-tuned than heart or throat of dove,
Soul into soul, song into song,
Life changing into life, by laws that work not wrong;

XXV

O natural force in spirit and sense, that art
One thing in all things, fruit of thine own fruit,
O thought illimitable and infinite heart
Whose blood is life in limbs indissolute
That still keeps hurtless thine invisible part
And inextirpable thy viewless root
Whence all sweet shafts of green and each thy dart
Of sharpening leaf and bud resundering shoot;
Hills that the day-star hails,
Heights that the first beam scales,
And heights that souls outshining suns salute,
Valleys for each mouth born
Free now of plenteous corn,
Waters and woodlands' musical or mute;
Free winds that brighten brows as free,
And thunder and laughter and lightning of the sovereign sea;

XXVI

Rivers and springs, and storms that seek your prey;
With strong wings ravening through the skies by night;
Spirits and stars that hold one choral way;
O light of heaven, and thou the heavenlier light
Aflame above the souls of men that sway
All generations of all years with might;
O sunrise of the repossessing day,
And sunrise of all-renovating right;

And thou, whose trackless foot
Mocks hope's or fear's pursuit,
Swift Revolution, changing depth with height;
And thou, whose mouth makes one
All songs that seek the sun,
Serene Republic of a world made white;
Thou, Freedom, whence the soul's springs ran;
Praise earth for man's sake living, and for earth's sake man.

XXVII

Make yourselves wings, O tarrying feet of fate,
And hidden hour that hast our hope to bear,
A child-god, through the morning-coloured gate
That lets love in upon the golden air,
Dead on whose threshold lies heart-broken hate,
Dead discord, dead injustice, dead despair;
O love long looked for, wherefore wilt thou wait,
And shew not yet the dawn on thy bright hair.
Not yet thine hand released
Refreshing the faint east,
Thine hand reconquering heaven, to seat man there?
Come forth, be born and live,
Thou that hast help to give
And light to make man's day of manhood fair:
With flight outflying the sphered sun,
Hasten thine hour and halt not, till thy work be done.

A WATCH IN THE NIGHT

I

Watchman, what of the night?—
Storm and thunder and rain,
Lights that waver and wane,
Leaving the watchfires unlit.
Only the balefires are bright,
And the flash of the lamps now and then
From a palace where spoilers sit,
Trampling the children of men.

II

Prophet, what of the night?—

I stand by the verge of the sea,
Banished, uncomforted, free,
Hearing the noise of the waves
And sudden flashes that smite
Some man's tyrannous head,
Thundering, heard among graves
That hide the hosts of his dead.

III

Mourners, what of the night?—
All night through without sleep
We weep, and we weep, and we weep.
Who shall give us our sons?
Beaks of raven and kite,
Mouths of wolf and of hound,
Give us them back whom the guns
Shot for you dead on the ground.

IV

Dead men, what of the night?—
Cannon and scaffold and sword,
Horror of gibbet and cord,
Mowed us as sheaves for the grave,
Mowed us down for the right.
We do not grudge or repent.
Freely to freedom we gave
Pledges, till life should be spent.

V

Statesman, what of the night?—
The night will last me my time.
The gold on a crown or a crime
Looks well enough yet by the lamps.
Have we not fingers to write,
Lips to swear at a need?
Then, when danger decamps,
Bury the word with the deed.

VI

Warrior, what of the night?—

Whether it be not or be
Night, is as one thing to me.
I for one, at the least,
Ask not of dews if they blight,
Ask not of flames if they slay,
Ask not of prince or of priest
How long ere we put them away.

VII

Master, what of the night?—
Child, night is not at all
Anywhere, fallen or to fall,
Save in our star-stricken eyes.
Forth of our eyes it takes flight,
Look we but once nor before
Nor behind us, but straight on the skies;
Night is not then any more.

VIII

Exile, what of the night?—
The tides and the hours run out,
The seasons of death and of doubt,
The night-watches bitter and sore.
In the quicksands leftward and right
My feet sink down under me;
But I know the scents of the shore
And the broad blown breaths of the sea.

IX

Captives, what of the night?—
It rains outside overhead
Always, a rain that is red,
And our faces are soiled with the rain.
Here in the seasons' despite
Day-time and night-time are one,
Till the curse of the kings and the chain
Break, and their toils be undone.

X

Christian, what of the night?—

I cannot tell; I am blind.
I halt and hearken behind
If haply the hours will go back
And return to the dear dead light,
To the watchfires and stars that of old
Shone where the sky now is black,
Glowed where the earth now is cold.

High priest, what of the night?—
The night is horrible here
With haggard faces and fear,
Blood, and the burning of fire.
Mine eyes are emptied of sight,
Mine hands are full of the dust.
If the God of my faith be a liar,
Who is it that I shall trust?

Princes, what of the night?—
Night with pestilent breath
Feeds us, children of death,
Clothes us close with her gloom.
Rapine and famine and fright
Crouch at our feet and are fed.
Earth where we pass is a tomb,
Life where we triumph is dead.

Martyrs, what of the night?—
Nay, is it night with you yet?
We, for our part, we forget
What night was, if it were.
The loud red mouths of the fight
Are silent and shut where we are.
In our eyes the tempestuous air
Shines as the face of a star.

England, what of the night?—

Night is for slumber and sleep,
Warm, no season to weep.
Let me alone till the day.
Sleep would I still if I might,
Who have slept for two hundred years.
Once I had honour, they say;
But slumber is sweeter than tears.

XV

France, what of the night?—
Night is the prostitute's noon,
Kissed and drugged till she swoon,
Spat upon, trod upon, whored.
With bloodred rose-garlands dight,
Round me reels in the dance
Death, my saviour, my lord,
Crowned; there is no more France.

XVI

Italy, what of the night?—
Ah, child, child, it is long!
Moonbeam and starbeam and song
Leave it dumb now and dark.
Yet I perceive on the height
Eastward, not now very far,
A song too loud for the lark,
A light too strong for a star.

XVII

Germany, what of the night?—
Long has it lulled me with dreams;
Now at midwatch, as it seems,
Light is brought back to mine eyes,
And the mastery of old and the might
Lives in the joints of mine hands,
Steadies my limbs as they rise,
Strengthens my foot as it stands.

XVIII

Europe, what of the night?—

Ask of heaven, and the sea,
And my babes on the bosom of me,
Nations of mine, but ungrown.
There is one who shall surely requite
All that endure or that err:
She can answer alone:
Ask not of me, but of her.

XIX

Liberty, what of the night?—
I feel not the red rains fall,
Hear not the tempest at all,
Nor thunder in heaven any more.
All the distance is white
With the soundless feet of the sun.
Night, with the woes that it wore,
Night is over and done.

SUPER FLUMINA BABYLONIS

By the waters of Babylon we sat down and wept,
Remembering thee,
That for ages of agony hast endured, and slept,
And wouldst not see.
By the waters of Babylon we stood up and sang,
Considering thee,
That a blast of deliverance in the darkness rang,
To set thee free.

And with trumpets and thunderings and with morning song
Came up the light;
And thy spirit uplifted thee to forget thy wrong
As day doth night.

And thy sons were dejected not any more, as then
When thou wast shamed;
When thy lovers went heavily without heart, as men
Whose life was maimed.

In the desolate distances, with a great desire,
For thy love's sake,
With our hearts going back to thee, they were filled with fire,
Were nigh to break.

It was said to us: "Verily ye are great of heart,
But ye shall bend;
Ye are bondmen and bondwomen, to be scourged and smart,
To toil and tend."

And with harrows men harrowed us, and subdued with spears,
And crushed with shame;
And the summer and winter was, and the length of years,
And no change came.

By the rivers of Italy, by the sacred streams,
By town, by tower,
There was feasting with revelling, there was sleep with dreams,
Until thine hour.

And they slept and they rioted on their rose-hung beds,
With mouths on flame,
And with love-locks vine-chapleted, and with rose-crowned heads
And robes of shame.

And they knew not their forefathers, nor the hills and streams
And words of power,
Nor the gods that were good to them, but with songs and dreams
Filled up their hour.

By the rivers of Italy, by the dry streams' beds,
When thy time came,
There was casting of crowns from them, from their young men's heads,
The crowns of shame.

By the horn of Eridanus, by the Tiber mouth,
As thy day rose,
They arose up and girded them to the north and south,
By seas, by snows.

As a water in January the frost confines,
Thy kings bound thee;
As a water in April is, in the new-blown vines,
Thy sons made free.

And thy lovers that looked for thee, and that mourned from far,
For thy sake dead,
We rejoiced in the light of thee, in the signal star
Above thine head.

In thy grief had we followed thee, in thy passion loved,
Loved in thy loss;
In thy shame we stood fast to thee, with thy pangs were moved,

Clung to thy cross.

By the hillside of Calvary we beheld thy blood,
Thy bloodred tears,
As a mother's in bitterness, an unebbing flood,
Years upon years.

And the north was Gethsemane, without leaf or bloom,
A garden sealed;
And the south was Aceldama, for a sanguine fume
Hid all the field.

By the stone of the sepulchre we returned to weep,
From far, from prison;
And the guards by it keeping it we beheld asleep,
But thou wast risen.

And an angel's similitude by the unsealed grave,
And by the stone:
And the voice was angelical, to whose words God gave
Strength like his own.

"Lo, the graveclothes of Italy that are folded up
In the grave's gloom!
And the guards as men wrought upon with a charmed cup,
By the open tomb.

"And her body most beautiful, and her shining head,
These are not here;
For your mother, for Italy, is not surely dead:
Have ye no fear.

"As of old time she spake to you, and you hardly heard,
Hardly took heed,
So now also she saith to you, yet another word,
Who is risen indeed.

"By my saying she saith to you, in your ears she saith,
Who hear these things,
Put no trust in men's royalties, nor in great men's breath,
Nor words of kings.

"For the life of them vanishes and is no more seen,
Nor no more known;
Nor shall any remember him if a crown hath been,
Or where a throne.

"Unto each man his handiwork, unto each his crown,

The just Fate gives;
Whoso takes the world's life on him and his own lays down,
He, dying so, lives.

"Whoso bears the whole heaviness of the wronged world's weight
And puts it by,
It is well with him suffering, though he face man's fate;
How should he die?

"Seeing death has no part in him any more, no power
Upon his head;
He has bought his eternity with a little hour,
And is not dead.

"For an hour, if ye look for him, he is no more found,
For one hour's space;
Then ye lift up your eyes to him and behold him crowned,
A deathless face.

"On the mountains of memory, by the world's wellsprings,
In all men's eyes,
Where the light of the life of him is on all past things,
Death only dies.

"Not the light that was quenched for us, nor the deeds that were,
Nor the ancient days,
Nor the sorrows not sorrowful, nor the face most fair
Of perfect praise."

So the angel of Italy's resurrection said,
So yet he saith;
So the son of her suffering, that from breasts nigh dead
Drew life, not death.

That the pavement of Golgotha should be white as snow,
Not red, but white;
That the waters of Babylon should no longer flow,
And men see light.

THE HALT BEFORE ROME

September 1867

Is it so, that the sword is broken,
Our sword, that was halfway drawn?
Is it so, that the light was a spark,

That the bird we hailed as the lark
Sang in her sleep in the dark,
And the song we took for a token
Bore false witness of dawn?
Spread in the sight of the lion,
Surely, we said, is the net
Spread but in vain, and the snare
Vain; for the light is aware,
And the common, the chainless air,
Of his coming whom all we cry on;
Surely in vain is it set.

Surely the day is on our side,
And heaven, and the sacred sun;
Surely the stars, and the bright
Immemorial inscrutable night:
Yea, the darkness, because of our light,`
Is no darkness, but blooms as a bower-side
When the winter is over and done;

Blooms underfoot with young grasses
Green, and with leaves overhead,
Windflowers white, and the low
New-dropped blossoms of snow;
And or ever the May winds blow,
And or ever the March wind passes,
Flames with anemones red.

We are here in the world's bower-garden,
We that have watched out the snow.
Surely the fruitfuller showers,
The splendider sunbeams are ours;
Shall winter return on the flowers,
And the frost after April harden,
And the fountains in May not flow?

We have in our hands the shining
And the fire in our hearts of a star.
Who are we that our tongues should palter,
Hearts bow down, hands falter,
Who are clothed as with flame from the altar,
That the kings of the earth, repining,
Far off, watch from afar?

Woe is ours if we doubt or dissemble,
Woe, if our hearts not abide.
Are our chiefs not among us, we said,
Great chiefs, living and dead,

To lead us glad to be led?
For whose sake, if a man of us tremble,
He shall not be on our side.

What matter if these lands tarry,
That tarried (we said) not of old?
France, made drunken by fate,
England, that bore up the weight
Once of men's freedom, a freight
Holy, but heavy to carry
For hands overflowing with gold.

Though this be lame, and the other
Fleet, but blind from the sun,
And the race be no more to these,
Alas! nor the palm to seize,
Who are weary and hungry of ease,
Yet, O Freedom, we said, O our mother,
Is there not left to thee one?

Is there not left of thy daughters,
Is there not one to thine hand?
Fairer than these, and of fame
Higher from of old by her name;
Washed in her tears, and in flame
Bathed as in baptism of waters,
Unto all men a chosen land.

Her hope in her heart was broken,
Fire was upon her, and clomb,
Hiding her, high as her head;
And the world went past her, and said
(We heard it say) she was dead;
And now, behold, she bath spoken,
She that was dead, saying, "Rome."

O mother of all men's nations,
Thou knowest if the deaf world heard!
Heard not now to her lowest
Depths, where the strong blood slowest
Beats at her bosom, thou knowest,
In her toils, in her dim tribulations,
Rejoiced not, hearing the word.

The sorrowful, bound unto sorrow,
The woe-worn people, and all
That of old were discomforted,
And men that famish for bread,

And men that mourn for their dead,
She bade them be glad on the morrow,
Who endured in the day of her thrall.

The blind, and the people in prison,
Souls without hope, without home,
How glad were they all that heard!
When the winged white flame of the word
Passed over men's dust, and stirred
Death; for Italia was risen,
And risen her light upon Rome.

The light of her sword in the gateway
Shone, an unquenchable flame,
Bloodless, a sword to release,
A light from the eyes of peace,
To bid grief utterly cease,
And the wrong of the old world straightway
Pass from the face of her fame:

Hers, whom we turn to and cry on,
Italy, mother of men:
From the light of the face of her glory,
At the sound of the storm of her story,
That the sanguine shadows and hoary
Should flee from the foot of the lion,
Lion-like, forth of his den.

As the answering of thunder to thunder
Is the storm-beaten sound of her past;
As the calling of sea unto sea
Is the noise of her years yet to be;
For this ye knew not is she,
Whose bonds are broken in sunder;
This is she at the last.

So spake we aloud, high-minded,
Full of our will; and behold,
The speech that was halfway spoken
Breaks, as a pledge that is broken,
As a king's pledge, leaving in token
Grief only for high hopes blinded,
New grief grafted on old.

We halt by the walls of the city,
Within sound of the clash of her chain.
Hearing, we know that in there
The lioness chafes in her lair,

Shakes the storm of her hair,
Struggles in hands without pity,
Roars to the lion in vain.

Whose hand is stretched forth upon her?
Whose curb is white with her foam?
Clothed with the cloud of his deeds,
Swathed in the shroud of his creeds,
Who is this that has trapped her and leads,
Who turns to despair and dishonour
Her name, her name that was Rome?

Over fields without harvest or culture,
Over hordes without honour or love,
Over nations that groan with their kings,
As an imminent pestilence flings
Swift death from her shadowing wings,
So he, who hath claws as a vulture,
Plumage and beak as a dove.

He saith, "I am pilot and haven,
Light and redemption I am
Unto souls overlaboured," he saith;
And to all men the blast of his breath
Is a savour of death unto death;
And the Dove of his worship a raven,
And a wolf-cub the life-giving Lamb.

He calls his sheep as a shepherd,
Calls from the wilderness home,
"Come unto me and be fed,"
To feed them with ashes for bread
And grass from the graves of the dead,
Leaps on the fold as a leopard,
Slays, and says, "I am Rome,"

Rome, having rent her in sunder,
With the clasp of an adder he clasps;
Swift to shed blood are his feet,
And his lips, that have man for their meat,
Smoother than oil, and more sweet
Than honey, but hidden thereunder
Festers the poison of asps.

As swords are his tender mercies,
His kisses as mortal stings;
Under his hallowing hands
Life dies down in all lands;

Kings pray to him, prone where he stands,
And his blessings, as other men's curses,
Disanoint where they consecrate kings.

With an oil of unclean consecration,
With effusion of blood and of tears,
With uplifting of cross and of keys,
Priest, though thou hallow us these,
Yet even as they cling to thy knees
Nation awakens by nation,
King by king disappears.

How shall the spirit be loyal
To the shell of a spiritless thing?
Erred once, in only a word,
The sweet great song that we heard
Poured upon Tuscany, erred,
Calling a crowned man royal
That was no more than a king.

Sea-eagle of English feather,
A song-bird beautiful-souled,
She knew not them that she sang;
The golden trumpet that rang
From Florence, in vain for them, sprang
As a note in the nightingales' weather
Far over Fiesole rolled.

She saw not—happy, not seeing—
Saw not as we with her eyes
Aspromonte; she felt
Never the heart in her melt
As in us when the news was dealt
Melted all hope out of being,
Dropped all dawn from the skies.

In that weary funereal season,
In that heart-stricken grief-ridden time,
The weight of a king and the worth,
With anger and sorrowful mirth,
We weighed in the balance of earth,
And light was his word as a treason,
And heavy his crown as a crime.

Banners of kings shall ye follow
None, and have thrones on your side
None; ye shall gather and grow
Silently, row upon row,

Chosen of Freedom to go
Gladly where darkness may swallow,
Gladly where death may divide.

Have we not men with us royal,
Men the masters of things?
In the days when our life is made new,
All souls perfect and true
Shall adore whom their forefathers slew;
And these indeed shall be loyal,
And those indeed shall be kings.

Yet for a space they abide with us,
Yet for a little they stand,
Bearing the heat of the day.
When their presence is taken away,
We shall wonder and worship, and say,
"Was not a star on our side with us?
Was not a God at our hand?"

These, O men, shall ye honour,
Liberty only, and these.
For thy sake and for all men's and mine,
Brother, the crowns of them shine
Lighting the way to her shrine,
That our eyes may be fastened upon her,
That our hands may encompass her knees.

In this day is the sign of her shown to you;
Choose ye, to live or to die,
Now is her harvest in hand;
Now is her light in the land;
Choose ye, to sink or to stand,
For the might of her strength is made known to you
Now, and her arm is on high.

Serve not for any man's wages,
Pleasure nor glory nor gold;
Not by her side are they won
Who saith unto each of you, "Son,
Silver and gold have I none;
I give but the love of all ages,
And the life of my people of old."

Fear not for any man's terrors;
Wait not for any man's word;
Patiently, each in his place,
Gird up your loins to the race;

Following the print of her pace,
Purged of desires and of errors,
March to the tune ye have heard.

March to the tune of the voice of her,
Breathing the balm of her breath,
Loving the light of her skies.
Blessed is he on whose eyes
Dawns but her light as he dies;
Blessed are ye that make choice of her,
Equal to life and to death.

Ye that when faith is nigh frozen,
Ye that when hope is nigh gone,
Still, over wastes, over waves,
Still, among wrecks, among graves,
Follow the splendour that saves,
Happy, her children, her chosen,
Loyally led of her on.

The sheep of the priests, and the cattle
That feed in the penfolds of kings,
Sleek is their flock and well-fed;
Hardly she giveth you bread,
Hardly a rest for the head,
Till the day of the blast of the battle
And the storm of the wind of her wings.

Ye that have joy in your living,
Ye that are careful to live,
You her thunders go by:
Live, let men be, let them lie,
Serve your season, and die;
Gifts have your masters for giving,
Gifts hath not Freedom to give;

She, without shelter or station,
She, beyond limit or bar,
Urges to slumberless speed
Armies that famish, that bleed,
Sowing their lives for her seed,
That their dust may rebuild her a nation,
That their souls may relight her a star.

Happy are all they that follow her;
Them shall no trouble cast down;
Though she slay them, yet shall they trust in her,
For unsure there is nought nor unjust in her,

Blemish is none, neither rust in her;
Though it threaten, the night shall not swallow her,
Tempest and storm shall not drown.

Hither, O strangers, that cry for her,
Holding your lives in your hands,
Hither, for here is your light,
Where Italy is, and her might;
Strength shall be given you to fight,
Grace shall be given you to die for her,
For the flower, for the lady of lands;

Turn ye, whose anguish oppressing you
Crushes, asleep and awake,
For the wrong which is wrought as of yore;
That Italia may give of her store,
Having these things to give and no more;
Only her hands on you, blessing you;
Only a pang for her sake;

Only her bosom to die on;
Only her heart for a home,
And a name with her children to be
From Calabrian to Adrian sea
Famous in cities made free
That ring to the roar of the lion
Proclaiming republican Rome.

MENTANA: FIRST ANNIVERSARY

At the time when the stars are grey,
And the gold of the molten moon
Fades, and the twilight is thinned,
And the sun leaps up, and the wind,
A light rose, not of the day,
A stronger light than of noon.
As the light of a face much loved
Was the face of the light that clomb;
As a mother's whitened with woes
Her adorable head that arose;
As the sound of a God that is moved,
Her voice went forth upon Rome.

At her lips it fluttered and failed
Twice, and sobbed into song,
And sank as a flame sinks under;

Then spake, and the speech was thunder,
And the cheek as he heard it paled
Of the wrongdoer grown grey with the wrong.

"Is it time, is it time appointed,
Angel of time, is it near?
For the spent night aches into day
When the kings shall slay not or pray,
And the high-priest, accursed and anointed,
Sickens to deathward with fear.

"For the bones of my slain are stirred,
And the seed of my earth in her womb
Moves as the heart of a bud
Beating with odorous blood
To the tune of the loud first bird
Burns and yearns into bloom.

"I lay my hand on her bosom,
My hand on the heart of my earth,
And I feel as with shiver and sob
The triumphant heart in her throb,
The dead petals dilate into blossom,
The divine blood beat into birth.

"O my earth, are the springs in thee dry?
O sweet, is thy body a tomb?
Nay, springs out of springs derive,
And summers from summers alive,
And the living from them that die;
No tomb is here, but a womb.

"O manifold womb and divine,
Give me fruit of my children, give!
I have given thee my dew for thy root,
Give thou me for my mouth of thy fruit;
Thine are the dead that are mine,
And mine are thy sons that live.

"O goodly children, O strong
Italian spirits, that wear
My glories as garments about you,
Could time or the world misdoubt you,
Behold, in disproof of the wrong,
The field of the grave-pits there.

"And ye that fell upon sleep,
We have you too with us yet.

Fairer than life or than youth
Is this, to die for the truth:
No death can sink you so deep
As their graves whom their brethren forget.

"Were not your pains as my pains?
As my name are your names not divine?
Was not the light in your eyes
Mine, the light of my skies,
And the sweet shed blood of your veins,
O my beautiful martyrs, mine?

"Of mine earth were your dear limbs made,
Of mine air was your sweet life's breath;
At the breasts of my love ye were fed,
O my children, my chosen, my dead,
At my breasts where again ye are laid,
At the old mother's bosom, in death.

"But ye that live, O their brothers,
Be ye to me as they were;
Give me, my children that live,
What these dead grudged not to give,
Who alive were sons of your mother's,
Whose lips drew breath of your air.

"Till darkness by dawn be cloven,
Let youth's self mourn and abstain;
And love's self find not an hour,
And spring's self wear not a flower,
And Lycoris, with hair unenwoven,
Hail back to the banquet in vain.

"So sooner and surer the glory
That is not with us shall be,
And stronger the hands that smite
The heads of the sons of night,
And the sound throughout earth of our story
Give all men heart to be free."

BLESSED AMONG WOMEN

To the Signora Cairoli

I
Blessed was she that bare,

Hidden in flesh most fair,
For all men's sake the likeness of all love;
Holy that virgin's womb,
The old record saith, on whom
The glory of God alighted as a dove;
Blessed, who brought to gracious birth
The sweet-souled Saviour of a man-tormented earth.

II

But four times art thou blest,
At whose most holy breast
Four times a godlike soldier-saviour hung;
And thence a fourfold Christ
Given to be sacrificed
To the same cross as the same bosom clung;
Poured the same blood, to leave the same
Light on the many-folded mountain-skirts of fame.

III

Shall they and thou not live,
The children thou didst give
Forth of thine hands, a godlike gift, to death,
Through fire of death to pass
For her high sake that was
Thine and their mother, that gave all you breath?
Shall ye not live till time drop dead,
O mother, and each her children's consecrated head?

IV

Many brought gifts to take
For her love's supreme sake,
Life and life's love, pleasure and praise and rest,
And went forth bare; but thou,
So much once richer, and now
Poorer than all these, more than these be blest;
Poorer so much, by so much given,
Than who gives earth for heaven's sake, not for earth's sake heaven.

V

Somewhat could each soul save,

What thing soever it gave,
But thine, mother, what has thy soul kept back?
None of thine all, not one,
To serve thee and be thy son,
Feed with love all thy days, lest one day lack;
All thy whole life's love, thine heart's whole,
Thou hast given as who gives gladly, O thou the supreme soul.

VI

The heart's pure flesh and blood,
The heaven thy motherhood,
The live lips, the live eyes, that lived on thee;
The hands that clove with sweet
Blind clutch to thine, the feet
That felt on earth their first way to thy knee;
The little laughter of mouths milk-fed,
Now open again to feed on dust among the dead;

VII

The fair, strong, young men's strength,
Light of life-days and length,
And glory of earth seen under and stars above,
And years that bring to tame
Now the wild falcon fame,
Now, to stroke smooth, the dove-white breast of love;
The life unlived, the unsown seeds,
Suns unbeholden, songs unsung, and undone deeds.

VIII

Therefore shall man's love be
As an own son to thee,
And the world's worship of thee for a child;
All thine own land as one
New-born, a nursing son,
All thine own people a new birth undefiled;
And all the unborn Italian time,
And all its glory, and all its works, thy seed sublime.

IX

That henceforth no man's breath,

Saying "Italy," but saith
In that most sovereign word thine equal name;
Nor can one speak of thee
But he saith "Italy,"
Seeing in two suns one co-eternal flame;
One heat, one heaven, one heart, one fire,
One light, one love, one benediction, one desire.

X

Blest above praise and prayer
And incense of men's air,
Thy place is higher than where such voices rise
As in men's temples make
Music for some vain sake,
This God's or that God's, in one weary wise;
Thee the soul silent, the shut heart,
The locked lips of the spirit praise thee that thou art.

XI

Yea, for man's whole life's length,
And with man's whole soul's strength,
We praise thee, O holy, and bless thee, O mother of lights;
And send forth as on wings
The world's heart's thanksgivings,
Song-birds to sing thy days through and thy nights;
And wrap thee around and arch thee above
With the air of benediction and the heaven of love.

XII

And toward thee our unbreathed words
Fly speechless, winged as birds,
As the Indian flock, children of Paradise,
The winged things without feet,
Fed with God's dew for meat,
That live in the air and light of the utter skies;
So fleet, so flying a footless flight,
With wings for feet love seeks thee, to partake thy sight.

XIII

Love like a clear sky spread

Bends over thy loved head,
As a new heaven bends over a new-born earth,
When the old night's womb is great
With young stars passionate
And fair new planets fiery-fresh from birth;
And moon-white here, there hot like Mars,
Souls that are worlds shine on thee, spirits that are stars.

Till the whole sky burns through
With heaven's own heart-deep hue,
With passion-coloured glories of lit souls;
And thine above all names
Writ highest with lettering flames
Lightens, and all the old starriest aureoles
And all the old holiest memories wane,
And the old names of love's chosen, found in thy sight vain.

And crowned heads are discrowned,
And stars sink without sound,
And love's self for thy love's sake waxes pale
Seeing from his storied skies
In what new reverent wise
Thee Rome's most highest, her sovereign daughters, hail;
Thee Portia, thee Veturia grey,
Thee Arria, thee Cornelia, Roman more than they.

Even all these as all we
Subdue themselves to thee,
Bow their heads haloed, quench their fiery fame;
Seen through dim years divine,
Their faint lights feminine
Sink, then spring up rekindled from thy flame;
Fade, then reflower and reillume
From thy fresh spring their wintering age with new-blown bloom.

To thy much holier head

Even theirs, the holy and dead,
Bow themselves each one from her heavenward height;
Each in her shining turn,
All tremble toward thee and yearn
To melt in thine their consummated light;
Till from day's Capitolian dome
One glory of many glories lighten upon Rome.

XVIII

Hush thyself, song, and cease,
Close, lips, and hold your peace;
What help hast thou, what part have ye herein?
But you, with sweet shut eyes,
Heart-hidden memories,
Dreams and dumb thoughts that keep what things have been
Silent, and pure of all words said,
Praise without song the living, without dirge the dead.

XIX

Thou, strengthless in these things,
Song, fold thy feebler wings,
And as a pilgrim go forth girt and shod,
And where the new graves are,
And where the sunset star,
To the pure spirit of man that men call God,
To the high soul of things, that is
Made of men's heavenlier hopes and mightier memories;

XX

To the elements that make
For the soul's living sake
This raiment of dead things, of shadow and trance,
That give us chance and time
Wherein to aspire and climb
And set our life's work higher than time or chance
The old sacred elements, that give
The breath of life to days that die, to deeds that live;

XXI

To them, veiled gods and great,

There bow thee and dedicate
The speechless spirit in these thy weak words hidden;
And mix thy reverent breath
With holier air of death,
At the high feast of sorrow a guest unbidden,
Till with divine triumphal tears
Thou fill men's eyes who listen with a heart that hears.

THE LITANY OF NATIONS

μᾶ τᾶ, μᾶ τᾶ, βοὰν
φοβερὸν ἀπότρεπε.
AESCH. Supp. 890.

CHORUS

If with voice of words or prayers thy sons may reach thee,
We thy latter sons, the men thine after-birth,
We the children of thy grey-grown age, O Earth,
O our mother everlasting, we beseech thee,
By the sealed and secret ages of thy life;
By the darkness wherein grew thy sacred forces;
By the songs of stars thy sisters in their courses;
By thine own song hoarse and hollow and shrill with strife;
By thy voice distuned and marred of modulation;
By the discord of thy measure's march with theirs;
By the beauties of thy bosom, and the cares;
By thy glory of growth, and splendour of thy station;
By the shame of men thy children, and the pride;
By the pale-cheeked hope that sleeps and weeps and passes,
As the grey dew from the morning mountain-grasses;
By the white-lipped sightless memories that abide;
By the silence and the sound of many sorrows;
By the joys that leapt up living and fell dead;
By the veil that hides thy hands and breasts and head,
Wrought of divers-coloured days and nights and morrows;
Isis, thou that knowest of God what worlds are worth,
Thou the ghost of God, the mother uncreated,
Soul for whom the floating forceless ages waited
As our forceless fancies wait on thee, O Earth;
Thou the body and soul, the father-God and mother,
If at all it move thee, knowing of all things done
Here where evil things and good things are not one,
But their faces are as fire against each other;
By thy morning and thine evening, night and day;
By the first white light that stirs and strives and hovers
As a bird above the brood her bosom covers,

By the sweet last star that takes the westward way;
By the night whose feet are shod with snow or thunder,
Fledged with plumes of storm, or soundless as the dew;
By the vesture bound of many-folded blue
Round her breathless breasts, and all the woven wonder;
By the golden-growing eastern stream of sea;
By the sounds of sunrise moving in the mountains;
By the forces of the floods and unsealed fountains;
Thou that badest man be born, bid man be free.

GREECE

I am she that made thee lovely with my beauty
From north to south:
Mine, the fairest lips, took first the fire of duty
From thine own mouth.
Mine, the fairest eyes, sought first thy laws and knew them
Truths undefiled;
Mine, the fairest hands, took freedom first into them,
A weanling child.
By my light, now he lies sleeping, seen above him
Where none sees other;
By my dead that loved and living men that love him;

CHORUS

Hear us, O mother.

ITALY

I am she that was the light of thee enkindled
When Greece grew dim;
She whose life grew up with man's free life, and dwindled
With wane of him.
She that once by sword and once by word imperial
Struck bright thy gloom;
And a third time, casting off these years funereal,
Shall burst thy tomb.
By that bond 'twixt thee and me whereat affrighted
Thy tyrants fear us;
By that hope and this remembrance reunited;

CHORUS

O mother, hear us.

PAIN

I am she that set my seal upon the nameless
West worlds of seas;
And my sons as brides took unto them the tameless
Hesperides.
Till my sins and sons through sinless lands dispersed,

With red flame shod,
Made accurst the name of man, and thrice accursed
The name of God.
Lest for those past fires the fires of my repentance
Hell's fume yet smother,
Now my blood would buy remission of my sentence;

CHORUS
O mother, hear us.

FRANCE
I am she that was thy sign and standard-bearer,
Thy voice and cry;
She that washed thee with her blood and left thee fairer,
The same was I.
Were not these the hands that raised thee fallen and fed thee,
These hands defiled?
Was not I thy tongue that spake, thine eye that led thee,
Not I thy child?
By the darkness on our dreams, and the dead errors
Of dead times near us;
By the hopes that hang around thee, and the terrors;

CHORUS
O mother, hear us.

RUSSIA
I am she whose hands are strong and her eyes blinded
And lips athirst
Till upon the night of nations many-minded
One bright day burst:
Till the myriad stars be molten into one light,
And that light thine;
Till the soul of man be parcel of the sunlight,
And thine of mine.
By the snows that blanch not him nor cleanse from slaughter
Who slays his brother;
By the stains and by the chains on me thy daughter;

CHORUS
O mother, hear us.

SWITZERLAND
I am she that shews on mighty limbs and maiden
Nor chain nor stain;
For what blood can touch these hands with gold unladen,
These feet what chain?
By the surf of spears one shieldless bosom breasted

And was my shield,
Till the plume-plucked Austrian vulture-heads twin-crested
Twice drenched the field;
By the snows and souls untrampled and untroubled
That shine to cheer us,
Light of those to these responsive and redoubled;

CHORUS
O mother, hear us.

GERMANY
I am she beside whose forest-hidden fountains
Slept freedom armed,
By the magic born to music in my mountains
Heart-chained and charmed.
By those days the very dream whereof delivers
My soul from wrong;
By the sounds that make of all my ringing rivers
None knows what song;
By the many tribes and names of my division
One from another;
By the single eye of sun-compelling vision;

CHORUS
O mother, hear us.

ENGLAND
I am she that was and was not of thy chosen,
Free, and not free;
She that fed thy springs, till now her springs are frozen;
Yet I am she.
By the sea that clothed and sun that saw me splendid
And fame that crowned,
By the song-fires and the sword-fires mixed and blended
That robed me round;
By the star that Milton's soul for Shelley's lighted,
Whose rays insphere us;
By the beacon-bright Republic far-off sighted;

CHORUS
O mother, hear us.
Turn away from us the cross-blown blasts of error,
That drown each other;
Turn away the fearful cry, the loud-tongued terror,
O Earth, O mother.
Turn away their eyes who track, their hearts who follow,
The pathless past;
Shew the soul of man, as summer shews the swallow,

The way at last.
By the sloth of men that all too long endure men
On man to tread;
By the cry of men, the bitter cry of poor men
That faint for bread;
By the blood-sweat of the people in the garden
Inwalled of kings;
By his passion interceding for their pardon
Who do these things;
By the sightless souls and fleshless limbs that labour
For not their fruit;
By the foodless mouth with foodless heart for neighbour,
That, mad, is mute;
By the child that famine eats as worms the blossom
—Ah God, the child!
By the milkless lips that strain the bloodless bosom
Till woe runs wild;
By the pastures that give grass to feed the lamb in,
Where men lack meat;
By the cities clad with gold and shame and famine;
By field and street;
By the people, by the poor man, by the master
That men call slave;
By the cross-winds of defeat and of disaster,
By wreck, by wave;
By the helm that keeps us still to sunwards driving,
Still eastward bound,
Till, as night-watch ends, day burn on eyes reviving,
And land be found:
We thy children, that arraign not nor impeach thee
Though no star steer us,
By the waves that wash the morning we beseech thee,
O mother, hear us.

HERTHA

I am that which began;
Out of me the years roll;
Out of me God and man;
I am equal and whole;
God changes, and man, and the form of them bodily; I am the soul.
Before ever land was,
Before ever the sea,
Or soft hair of the grass,
Or fair limbs of the tree,
Or the flesh-coloured fruit of my branches, I was, and thy soul was in me.

First life on my sources
First drifted and swam;
Out of me are the forces
That save it or damn;
Out of me man and woman, and wild-beast and bird; before God was, I am.

Beside or above me
Nought is there to go;
Love or unlove me,
Unknow me or know,
I am that which unloves me and loves; I am stricken, and I am the blow.

I the mark that is missed
And the arrows that miss,
I the mouth that is kissed
And the breath in the kiss,
The search, and the sought, and the seeker, the soul and the body that is.

I am that thing which blesses
My spirit elate;
That which caresses
With hands uncreate
My limbs unbegotten that measure the length of the measure of fate.

But what thing dost thou now,
Looking Godward, to cry
"I am I, thou art thou,
I am low, thou art high"?
I am thou, whom thou seekest to find him; find thou but thyself, thou art I.

I the grain and the furrow,
The plough-cloven clod
And the ploughshare drawn thorough,
The germ and the sod,
The deed and the doer, the seed and the sower, the dust which is God.

Hast thou known how I fashioned thee,
Child, underground?
Fire that impassioned thee,
Iron that bound,
Dim changes of water, what thing of all these hast thou known of or found?

Canst thou say in thine heart
Thou hast seen with thine eyes
With what cunning of art
Thou wast wrought in what wise,
By what force of what stuff thou wast shapen, and shown on my breast to the skies?

Who hath given, who hath sold it thee,
Knowledge of me?
Hath the wilderness told it thee?
Hast thou learnt of the sea?
Hast thou communed in spirit with night? have the winds taken counsel with thee?

Have I set such a star
To show light on thy brow
That thou sawest from afar
What I show to thee now?
Have ye spoken as brethren together, the sun and the mountains and thou?

What is here, dost thou know it?
What was, hast thou known?
Prophet nor poet
Nor tripod nor throne
Nor spirit nor flesh can make answer, but only thy mother alone.

Mother, not maker,
Born, and not made;
Though her children forsake her,
Allured or afraid,
Praying prayers to the God of their fashion, she stirs not for all that have prayed.

A creed is a rod,
And a crown is of night;
But this thing is God,
To be man with thy might,
To grow straight in the strength of thy spirit, and live out thy life as the light.

I am in thee to save thee,
As my soul in thee saith;
Give thou as I gave thee,
Thy life-blood and breath,
Green leaves of thy labour, white flowers of thy thought, and red fruit of thy death,

Be the ways of thy giving
As mine were to thee;
The free life of thy living,
Be the gift of it free;
Not as servant to lord, nor as master to slave, shalt thou give thee to me.

O children of banishment,
Souls overcast,
Were the lights ye see vanish meant
Alway to last,
Ye would know not the sun overshining the shadows and stars overpast.

I that saw where ye trod
The dim paths of the night
Set the shadow called God
In your skies to give light;
But the morning of manhood is risen, and the shadowless soul is in sight.

The tree many-rooted
That swells to the sky
With frondage red-fruited,
The life-tree am I;
In the buds of your lives is the sap of my leaves: ye shall live and not die.

But the Gods of your fashion
That take and that give,
In their pity and passion
That scourge and forgive,
They are worms that are bred in the bark that falls off; they shall die and not live.

My own blood is what stanches
The wounds in my bark;
Stars caught in my branches
Make day of the dark,
And are worshipped as suns till the sunrise shall tread out their fires as a spark.

Where dead ages hide under
The live roots of the tree,
In my darkness the thunder
Makes utterance of me;
In the clash of my boughs with each other ye hear the waves sound of the sea.

That noise is of Time,
As his feathers are spread
And his feet set to climb
Through the boughs overhead,
And my foliage rings round him and rustles, and branches are bent with his tread.

The storm-winds of ages
Blow through me and cease,
The war-wind that rages,
The spring-wind of peace,
Ere the breath of them roughen my tresses, ere one of my blossoms increase.

All sounds of all changes,
All shadows and lights
On the world's mountain-ranges
And stream-riven heights,
Whose tongue is the wind's tongue and language of storm-clouds on earth-shaking nights;

All forms of all faces,
All works of all hands
In unsearchable places
Of time-stricken lands,
All death and all life, and all reigns and all ruins, drop through me as sands.

Though sore be my burden
And more than ye know,
And my growth have no guerdon
But only to grow,
Yet I fail not of growing for lightnings above me or deathworms below.

These too have their part in me,
As I too in these;
Such fire is at heart in me,
Such sap is this tree's,
Which hath in it all sounds and all secrets of infinite lands and of seas.

In the spring-coloured hours
When my mind was as May's,
There brake forth of me flowers
By centuries of days,
Strong blossoms with perfume of manhood, shot out from my spirit as rays.

And the sound of them springing
And smell of their shoots
Were as warmth and sweet singing
And strength to my roots;
And the lives of my children made perfect with freedom of soul were my fruits.

I bid you but be;
I have need not of prayer;
I have need of you free
As your mouths of mine air;
That my heart may be greater within me, beholding the fruits of me fair.

More fair than strange fruit is
Of faiths ye espouse;
In me only the root is
That blooms in your boughs;
Behold now your God that ye made you, to feed him with faith of your vows.

In the darkening and whitening
Abysses adored,
With dayspring and lightning
For lamp and for sword,
God thunders in heaven, and his angels are red with the wrath of the Lord.

O my sons, O too dutiful
Toward Gods not of me,
Was not I enough beautiful?
Was it hard to be free?
For behold, I am with you, am in you and of you; look forth now and see.

Lo, winged with world's wonders,
With miracles shod,
With the fires of his thunders
For raiment and rod,
God trembles in heaven, and his angels are white with the terror of God.

For his twilight is come on him,
His anguish is here;
And his spirits gaze dumb on him,
Grown grey from his fear;
And his hour taketh hold on him stricken, the last of his infinite year.

Thought made him and breaks him,
Truth slays and forgives;
But to you, as time takes him,
This new thing it gives,
Even love, the beloved Republic, that feeds upon freedom and lives.

For truth only is living,
Truth only is whole,
And the love of his giving
Man's polestar and pole;
Man, pulse of my centre, and fruit of my body, and seed of my soul.

One birth of my bosom;
One beam of mine eye;
One topmost blossom
That scales the sky;
Man, equal and one with me, man that is made of me, man that is I.

BEFORE A CRUCIFIX

Here, down between the dusty trees,
At this lank edge of haggard wood,
Women with labour-loosened knees,
With gaunt backs bowed by servitude,
Stop, shift their loads, and pray, and fare
Forth with souls easier for the prayer.
The suns have branded black, the rains

Striped grey this piteous God of theirs;
The face is full of prayers and pains,
To which they bring their pains and prayers;
Lean limbs that shew the labouring bones,
And ghastly mouth that gapes and groans.

God of this grievous people, wrought
After the likeness of their race,
By faces like thine own besought,
Thine own blind helpless eyeless face,
I too, that have nor tongue nor knee
For prayer, I have a word to thee.

It was for this then, that thy speech
Was blown about the world in flame
And men's souls shot up out of reach
Of fear or lust or thwarting shame—
That thy faith over souls should pass
As sea-winds burning the grey grass?

It was for this, that prayers like these
Should spend themselves about thy feet,
And with hard overlaboured knees
Kneeling, these slaves of men should beat
Bosoms too lean to suckle sons
And fruitless as their orisons?

It was for this, that men should make
Thy name a fetter on men's necks,
Poor men's made poorer for thy sake,
And women's withered out of sex?
It was for this, that slaves should be,
Thy word was passed to set men free?

The nineteenth wave of the ages rolls
Now deathward since thy death and birth.
Hast thou fed full men's starved-out souls?
Hast thou brought freedom upon earth?
Or are there less oppressions done
In this wild world under the sun?

Nay, if indeed thou be not dead,
Before thy terrene shrine be shaken,
Look down, turn usward, bow thine head;
O thou that wast of God forsaken,
Look on thine household here, and see
These that have not forsaken thee.

Thy faith is fire upon their lips,
Thy kingdom golden in their hands;
They scourge us with thy words for whips,
They brand us with thy words for brands;
The thirst that made thy dry throat shrink
To their moist mouths commends the drink.

The toothed thorns that bit thy brows
Lighten the weight of gold on theirs;
Thy nakedness enrobes thy spouse
With the soft sanguine stuff she wears
Whose old limbs use for ointment yet
Thine agony and bloody sweat.

The blinding buffets on thine head
On their crowned heads confirm the crown;
Thy scourging dyes their raiment red,
And with thy bands they fasten down
For burial in the blood-bought field
The nations by thy stripes unhealed.

With iron for thy linen bands
And unclean cloths for winding-sheet
They bind the people's nail-pierced hands,
They hide the people's nail-pierced feet;
And what man or what angel known
Shall roll back the sepulchral stone?

But these have not the rich man's grave
To sleep in when their pain is done.
These were not fit for God to save.
As naked hell-fire is the sun
In their eyes living, and when dead
These have not where to lay their head.

They have no tomb to dig, and hide;
Earth is not theirs, that they should sleep.
On all these tombless crucified
No lovers' eyes have time to weep.
So still, for all man's tears and creeds,
The sacred body hangs and bleeds.

Through the left hand a nail is driven,
Faith, and another through the right,
Forged in the fires of hell and heaven,
Fear that puts out the eye of light:
And the feet soiled and scarred and pale
Are pierced with falsehood for a nail.

And priests against the mouth divine
Push their sponge full of poison yet
And bitter blood for myrrh and wine,
And on the same reed is it set
Wherewith before they buffeted
The people's disanointed head.

O sacred head, O desecrate,
O labour-wounded feet and hands,
O blood poured forth in pledge to fate
Of nameless lives in divers lands,
O slain and spent and sacrificed
People, the grey-grown speechless Christ!

Is there a gospel in the red
Old witness of thy wide-mouthed wounds?
From thy blind stricken tongueless head
What desolate evangel sounds
A hopeless note of hope deferred?
What word, if there be any word?

O son of man, beneath man's feet
Cast down, O common face of man
Whereon all blows and buffets meet,
O royal, O republican
Face of the people bruised and dumb
And longing till thy kingdom come!

The soldiers and the high priests part
Thy vesture: all thy days are priced,
And all the nights that eat thine heart.
And that one seamless coat of Christ,
The freedom of the natural soul,
They cast their lots for to keep whole.

No fragment of it save the name
They leave thee for a crown of scorns
Wherewith to mock thy naked shame
And forehead bitten through with thorns
And, marked with sanguine sweat and tears,
The stripes of eighteen hundred years

And we seek yet if God or man
Can loosen thee as Lazarus,
Bid thee rise up republican
And save thyself and all of us;
But no disciple's tongue can say

When thou shalt take our sins away.

And mouldering now and hoar with moss
Between us and the sunlight swings
The phantom of a Christless cross
Shadowing the sheltered heads of kings
And making with its moving shade
The souls of harmless men afraid.

It creaks and rocks to left and right
Consumed of rottenness and rust,
Worm-eaten of the worms of night,
Dead as their spirits who put trust,
Round its base muttering as they sit,
In the time-cankered name of it.

Thou, in the day that breaks thy prison,
People, though these men take thy name,
And hail and hymn thee rearisen,
Who made songs erewhile of thy shame,
Give thou not ear; for these are they
Whose good day was thine evil day.

Set not thine hand unto their cross.
Give not thy soul up sacrificed.
Change not the gold of faith for dross
Of Christian creeds that spit on Christ.
Let not thy tree of freedom be
Regrafted from that rotting tree.

This dead God here against my face
Hath help for no man; who hath seen
The good works of it, or such grace
As thy grace in it, Nazarene,
As that from thy live lips which ran
For man's sake, O thou son of man?

The tree of faith ingraffed by priests
Puts its foul foliage out above thee,
And round it feed man-eating beasts
Because of whom we dare not love thee;
Though hearts reach back and memories ache,
We cannot praise thee for their sake.

O hidden face of man, whereover
The years have woven a viewless veil,
If thou wast verily man's lover,
What did thy love or blood avail?

Thy blood the priests make poison of,
And in gold shekels coin thy love.

So when our souls look back to thee
They sicken, seeing against thy side,
Too foul to speak of or to see,
The leprous likeness of a bride,
Whose kissing lips through his lips grown
Leave their God rotten to the bone.

When we would see thee man, and know
What heart thou hadst toward men indeed,
Lo, thy blood-blackened altars; lo,
The lips of priests that pray and feed
While their own hell's worm curls and licks
The poison of the crucifix.

Thou bad'st let children come to thee;
What children now but curses come?
What manhood in that God can be
Who sees their worship, and is dumb?
No soul that lived, loved, wrought, and died,
Is this their carrion crucified.

Nay, if their God and thou be one,
If thou and this thing be the same,
Thou shouldst not look upon the sun;
The sun grows haggard at thy name.
Come down, be done with, cease, give o'er;
Hide thyself, strive not, be no more.

TENEBRÆ

At the chill high tide of the night,
At the turn of the fluctuant hours,
When the waters of time are at height,
In a vision arose on my sight
The kingdoms of earth and the powers.
In a dream without lightening of eyes
I saw them, children of earth,
Nations and races arise,
Each one after his wise,
Signed with the sign of his birth.

Sound was none of their feet,
Light was none of their faces;

In their lips breath was not, or heat,
But a subtle murmur and sweet
As of water in wan waste places.

Pale as from passionate years,
Years unassuaged of desire,
Sang they soft in mine ears,
Crowned with jewels of tears,
Girt with girdles of fire.

A slow song beaten and broken,
As it were from the dust and the dead,
As of spirits athirst unsloken,
As of things unspeakable spoken,
As of tears unendurable shed.

In the manifold sound remote,
In the molten murmur of song,
There was but a sharp sole note
Alive on the night and afloat,
The cry of the world's heart's wrong.

As the sea in the strait sea-caves,
The sound came straitened and strange;
A noise of the rending of graves,
A tidal thunder of waves,
The music of death and of change.

"We have waited so long," they say,
"For a sound of the God, for a breath,
For a ripple of the refluence of day,
For the fresh bright wind of the fray,
For the light of the sunrise of death.

"We have prayed not, we, to be strong,
To fulfil the desire of our eyes;
—Howbeit they have watched for it long,
Watched, and the night did them wrong,
Yet they say not of day, shall it rise?

"They are fearful and feeble with years,
Yet they doubt not of day if it be;
Yea, blinded and beaten with tears,
Yea, sick with foresight of fears,
Yet a little, and hardly, they see.

"We pray not, we, for the palm,
For the fruit ingraffed of the fight,

For the blossom of peace and the balm,
And the tender triumph and calm
Of crownless and weaponless right.

"We pray not, we, to behold
The latter august new birth,
The young day's purple and gold,
And divine, and rerisen as of old,
The sun-god Freedom on earth.

"Peace, and world's honour, and fame,
We have sought after none of these things;
The light of a life like flame
Passing, the storm of a name
Shaking the strongholds of kings:

"Nor, fashioned of fire and of air,
The splendour that burns on his head
Who was chiefest in ages that were,
Whose breath blew palaces bare,
Whose eye shone tyrannies dead:

"All these things in your day
Ye shall see, O our sons, and shall hold
Surely; but we, in the grey
Twilight, for one thing we pray,
In that day though our memories be cold:

"To feel on our brows as we wait
An air of the morning, a breath
From the springs of the east, from the gate
Whence freedom issues, and fate,
Sorrow, and triumph, and death

"From a land whereon time hath not trod,
Where the spirit is bondless and bare,
And the world's rein breaks, and the rod,
And the soul of a man, which is God,
He adores without altar or prayer:

For alone of herself and her right
She takes, and alone gives grace:
And the colours of things lose light,
And the forms, in the limitless white
Splendour of space without space:

"And the blossom of man from his tomb
Yearns open, the flower that survives;

And the shadows of changes consume
In the colourless passionate bloom
Of the live light made of our lives:

"Seeing each life given is a leaf
Of the manifold multiform flower,
And the least among these, and the chief,
As an ear in the red-ripe sheaf
Stored for the harvesting hour.

"O spirit of man, most holy,
The measure of things and the root,
In our summers and winters a lowly
Seed, putting forth of them slowly
Thy supreme blossom and fruit;

"In thy sacred and perfect year,
The souls that were parcel of thee
In the labour and life of us here
Shall be rays of thy sovereign sphere,
Springs of thy motion shall be.

"There is the fire that was man,
The light that was love, and the breath
That was hope ere deliverance began,
And the wind that was life for a span,
And the birth of new things, which is death

There, whosoever had light,
And, having, for men's sake gave;
All that warred against night;
All that were found in the fight
Swift to be slain and to save;

"Undisbranched of the storms that disroot us,
Of the lures that enthrall unenticed;
The names that exalt and transmute us;
The blood-bright splendour of Brutus,
The snow-bright splendour of Christ.

"There all chains are undone;
Day there seems but as night;
Spirit and sense are as one
In the light not of star nor of sun;
Liberty there is the light.

She, sole mother and maker,
Stronger than sorrow, than strife;

Deathless, though death overtake her;
Faithful, though faith should forsake her;
Spirit, and saviour, and life."

HYMN OF MAN

(During the Session in Rome of the Ecumenical Council)

In the grey beginning of years, in the twilight of things that began,
The word of the earth in the ears of the world, was it God? was it man?
The word of the earth to the spheres her sisters, the note of her song,
The sound of her speech in the ears of the starry and sisterly throng,
Was it praise or passion or prayer, was it love or devotion or dread,
When the veils of the shining air first wrapt her jubilant head?
When her eyes new-born of the night saw yet no star out of reach;
When her maiden mouth was alight with the flame of musical speech;
When her virgin feet were set on the terrible heavenly way,
And her virginal lids were wet with the dew of the birth of the day:
Eyes that had looked not on time, and ears that had heard not of death;
Lips that had learnt not the rhyme of change and passionate breath,
The rhythmic anguish of growth, and the motion of mutable things,
Of love that longs and is loth, and plume-plucked hope without wings,
Passions and pains without number, and life that runs and is lame,
From slumber again to slumber, the same race set for the same,
Where the runners outwear each other, but running with lampless hands
No man takes light from his brother till blind at the goal he stands:
Ah, did they know, did they dream of it, counting the cost and the worth?
The ways of her days, did they seem then good to the new-souled earth?
Did her heart rejoice, and the might of her spirit exult in her then,
Child yet no child of the night, and motherless mother of men?
Was it Love brake forth flower-fashion, a bird with gold on his wings,
Lovely, her firstborn passion, and impulse of firstborn things?
Was Love that nestling indeed that under the plumes of the night
Was hatched and hidden as seed in the furrow, and brought forth bright?
Was it Love lay shut in the shell world-shaped, having over him there
Black world-wide wings that impel the might of the night through air?
And bursting his shell as a bird, night shook through her sail-stretched vans,
And her heart as a water was stirred, and its heat was the firstborn man's.
For the waste of the dead void air took form of a world at birth,
And the waters and firmaments were, and light, and the life-giving earth.
The beautiful bird unbegotten that night brought forth without pain
In the fathomless years forgotten whereover the dead gods reign,
Was it love, life, godhead, or fate? we say the spirit is one
That moved on the dark to create out of darkness the stars and the sun.
Before the growth was the grower, and the seed ere the plant was sown;
But what was seed of the sower? and the grain of him, whence was it grown?

Foot after foot ye go back and travail and make yourselves mad;
Blind feet that feel for the track where highway is none to be had.
Therefore the God that ye make you is grievous, and gives not aid,
Because it is but for your sake that the God of your making is made.
Thou and I and he are not gods made men for a span,
But God, if a God there be, is the substance of men which is man.
Our lives are as pulses or pores of his manifold body and breath;
As waves of his sea on the shores where birth is the beacon of death.
We men, the multiform features of man, whatsoever we be,
Recreate him of whom we are creatures, and all we only are he.
Not each man of all men is God, but God is the fruit of the whole;
Indivisible spirit and blood, indiscernible body from soul.
Not men's but man's is the glory of godhead, the kingdom of time,
The mountainous ages made hoary with snows for the spirit to climb.
A God with the world inwound whose clay to his footsole clings;
A manifold God fast-bound as with iron of adverse things.
A soul that labours and lives, an emotion, a strenuous breath,
From the flame that its own mouth gives reillumed, and refreshed with death.
In the sea whereof centuries are waves the live God plunges and swims;
His bed is in all men's graves, but the worm hath not hold on his limbs.
Night puts out not his eyes, nor time sheds change on his head;
With such fire as the stars of the skies are the roots of his heart are fed.
Men are the thoughts passing through it, the veins that fulfil it with blood,
With spirit of sense to renew it as springs fulfilling a flood.
Men are the heartbeats of man, the plumes that feather his wings,
Storm-worn, since being began, with the wind and thunder of things.
Things are cruel and blind; their strength detains and deforms:
And the wearying wings of the mind still beat up the stream of their storms.
Still, as one swimming up stream, they strike out blind in the blast,
In thunders of vision and dream, and lightnings of future and past.
We are baffled and caught in the current and bruised upon edges of shoals;
As weeds or as reeds in the torrent of things are the wind-shaken souls.
Spirit by spirit goes under, a foam-bell's bubble of breath,
That blows and opens in sunder and blurs not the mirror of death.
For a worm or a thorn in his path is a man's soul quenched as a flame;
For his lust of an hour or his wrath shall the worm and the man be the same.
O God sore stricken of things! they have wrought him a raiment of pain;
Can a God shut eyelids and wings at a touch on the nerves of the brain?
O shamed and sorrowful God, whose force goes out at a blow!
What world shall shake at his nod? at his coming what wilderness glow?
What help in the work of his hands? what light in the track of his feet?
His days are snowflakes or sands, with cold to consume him and heat.
He is servant with Change for lord, and for wages he hath to his hire
Folly and force, and a sword that devours, and a ravening fire.
From the bed of his birth to his grave he is driven as a wind at their will;
Lest Change bow down as his slave, and the storm and the sword be still;
Lest earth spread open her wings to the sunward, and sing with the spheres;
Lest man be master of things, to prevail on their forces and fears.

By the spirit are things overcome; they are stark, and the spirit hath breath;
It hath speech, and their forces are dumb; it is living, and things are of death.
But they know not the spirit for master, they feel not force from above,
While man makes love to disaster, and woos desolation with love.
Yea, himself too hath made himself chains, and his own hands plucked out his eyes;
For his own soul only constrains him, his own mouth only denies.
The herds of kings and their hosts and the flocks of the high priests bow
To a master whose face is a ghost's; O thou that wast God, is it thou?
Thou madest man in the garden; thou temptedst man, and he fell;
Thou gavest him poison and pardon for blood and burnt-offering to sell.
Thou hast sealed thine elect to salvation, fast locked with faith for the key;
Make now for thyself expiation, and be thine atonement for thee.
Ah, thou that darkenest heaven—ah, thou that bringest a sword—
By the crimes of thine hands unforgiven they beseech thee to hear them, O Lord.
By the balefires of ages that burn for thine incense, by creed and by rood,
By the famine and passion that yearn and that hunger to find of thee food,
By the children that asked at thy throne of the priests that were fat with thine hire
For bread, and thou gavest a stone; for light, and thou madest them fire;
By the kiss of thy peace like a snake's kiss, that leaves the soul rotten at root;
By the savours of gibbets and stakes thou hast planted to bear to thee fruit;
By torture and terror and treason, that make to thee weapons and wings;
By thy power upon men for a season, made out of the malice of things;
O thou that hast built thee a shrine of the madness of man and his shame,
And hast hung in the midst for a sign of his worship the lamp of thy name;
That hast shown him for heaven in a vision a void world's shadow and shell,
And hast fed thy delight and derision with fire of belief as of hell;
That hast fleshed on the souls that believe thee the fang of the death-worm fear,
With anguish of dreams to deceive them whose faith cries out in thine ear;
By the face of the spirit confounded before thee and humbled in dust,
By the dread wherewith life was astounded and shamed out of sense of its trust,
By the scourges of doubt and repentance that fell on the soul at thy nod,
Thou art judged, O judge, and the sentence is gone forth against thee, O God.
Thy slave that slept is awake; thy slave but slept for a span;
Yea, man thy slave shall unmake thee, who made thee lord over man.
For his face is set to the east, his feet on the past and its dead;
The sun rearisen is his priest, and the heat thereof hallows his head.
His eyes take part in the morning; his spirit out-sounding the sea
Asks no more witness or warning from temple or tripod or tree.
He hath set the centuries at union; the night is afraid at his name;
Equal with life, in communion with death, he hath found them the same.
Past the wall unsurmounted that bars out our vision with iron and fire
He hath sent forth his soul for the stars to comply with and suns to conspire.
His thought takes flight for the centre wherethrough it hath part in the whole;
The abysses forbid it not enter: the stars make room for the soul.
Space is the soul's to inherit; the night is hers as the day;
Lo, saith man, this is my spirit; how shall not the worlds make way?
Space is thought's, and the wonders thereof, and the secret of space;
Is thought not more than the thunders and lightnings? shall thought give place?

Is the body not more than the vesture, the life not more than the meat?
The will than the word or the gesture, the heart than the hands or the feet?
Is the tongue not more than the speech is? the head not more than the crown?
And if higher than is heaven be the reach of the soul, shall not heaven bow down?
Time, father of life, and more great than the life it begat and began,
Earth's keeper and heaven's and their fate, lives, thinks, and hath substance in man.
Time's motion that throbs in his blood is the thought that gives heart to the skies,
And the springs of the fire that is food to the sunbeams are light to his eyes.
The minutes that beat with his heart are the words to which worlds keep chime,
And the thought in his pulses is part of the blood and the spirit of time.
He saith to the ages, Give; and his soul foregoes not her share;
Who are ye that forbid him to live, and would feed him with heavenlier air?
Will ye feed him with poisonous dust, and restore him with hemlock for drink,
Till he yield you his soul up in trust, and have heart not to know or to think?
He hath stirred him, and found out the flaw in his fetters, and cast them behind;
His soul to his soul is a law, and his mind is a light to his mind.
The seal of his knowledge is sure, the truth and his spirit are wed;
Men perish, but man shall endure; lives die, but the life is not dead.
He hath sight of the secrets of season, the roots of the years and the fruits;
His soul is at one with the reason of things that is sap to the roots.
He can hear in their changes a sound as the conscience of consonant spheres;
He can see through the years flowing round him the law lying under the years.
Who are ye that would bind him with curses and blind him with vapour of prayer?
Your might is as night that disperses when light is alive in the air.
The bow of your godhead is broken, the arm of your conquest is stayed;
Though ye call down God to bear token, for fear of you none is afraid.
Will ye turn back times, and the courses of stars, and the season of souls?
Shall God's breath dry up the sources that feed time full as it rolls?
Nay, cry on him then till he show you a sign, till he lift up a rod;
Hath he made not the nations to know him of old if indeed he be God?
Is no heat of him left in the ashes of thousands burnt up for his sake?
Can prayer not rekindle the flashes that shone in his face from the stake?
Cry aloud; for your God is a God and a Saviour; cry, make yourselves lean;
Is he drunk or asleep, that the rod of his wrath is unfelt and unseen?
Is the fire of his old loving-kindness gone out, that his pyres are acold?
Hath he gazed on himself unto blindness, who made men blind to behold?
Cry out, for his kingdom is shaken; cry out, for the people blaspheme;
Cry aloud till his godhead awaken; what doth he to sleep and to dream?
Cry, cut yourselves, gash you with knives and with scourges, heap on to you dust;
Is his life but as other gods' lives? is not this the Lord God of your trust?
Is not this the great God of your sires, that with souls and with bodies was fed,
And the world was on flame with his fires? O fools, he was God, and is dead.
He will hear not again the strong crying of earth in his ears as before,
And the fume of his multitudes dying shall flatter his nostrils no more.
By the spirit he ruled as his slave is he slain who was mighty to slay,
And the stone that is sealed on his grave he shall rise not and roll not away.
Yea, weep to him, lift up your hands; be your eyes as a fountain of tears;
Where he stood there is nothing that stands; if he call, there is no man that hears.

He hath doffed his king's raiment of lies now the wane of his kingdom is come;
Ears hath he, and hears not; and eyes, and he sees not; and mouth, and is dumb.
His red king's raiment is ripped from him naked, his staff broken down;
And the signs of his empire are stripped from him shuddering; and where is his crown?
And in vain by the wellsprings refrozen ye cry for the warmth of his sun—
O God, the Lord God of thy chosen, thy will in thy kingdom be done.
Kingdom and will hath he none in him left him, nor warmth in his breath;
Till his corpse be cast out of the sun will ye know not the truth of his death?
Surely, ye say, he is strong, though the times be against him and men;
Yet a little, ye say, and how long, till he come to show judgment again?
Shall God then die as the beasts die? who is it hath broken his rod?
O God, Lord God of thy priests, rise up now and show thyself God.
They cry out, thine elect, thine aspirants to heavenward, whose faith is as flame;
O thou the Lord God of our tyrants, they call thee, their God, by thy name.
By thy name that in hell-fire was written, and burned at the point of thy sword,
Thou art smitten, thou God, thou art smitten; thy death is upon thee, O Lord.
And the love-song of earth as thou diest resounds through the wind of her wings—
Glory to Man in the highest! for Man is the master of things.

THE PILGRIMS

Who is your lady of love, O ye that pass
Singing? and is it for sorrow of that which was
That ye sing sadly, or dream of what shall be?
For gladly at once and sadly it seems ye sing.
—Our lady of love by you is unbeholden;
For hands she hath none, nor eyes, nor lips, nor golden
Treasure of hair, nor face nor form; but we
That love, we know her more fair than anything.
—Is she a queen, having great gifts to give?
—Yea, these; that whoso hath seen her shall not live
Except he serve her sorrowing, with strange pain,
Travail and bloodshedding and bitterer tears;
And when she bids die he shall surely die.
And he shall leave all things under the sky
And go forth naked under sun and rain
And work and wait and watch out all his years.

—Hath she on earth no place of habitation?
—Age to age calling, nation answering nation,
Cries out, Where is she? and there is none to say;
For if she be not in the spirit of men,
For if in the inward soul she hath no place,
In vain they cry unto her, seeking her face,
In vain their mouths make much of her; for they
Cry with vain tongues, till the heart lives again.

—O ye that follow, and have ye no repentance?
For on your brows is written a mortal sentence,
An hieroglyph of sorrow, a fiery sign,
That in your lives ye shall not pause or rest,
Nor have the sure sweet common love, nor keep
Friends and safe days, nor joy of life nor sleep.
—These have we not, who have one thing, the divine
Face and clear eyes of faith and fruitful breast.

—And ye shall die before your thrones be won.
—Yea, and the changed world and the liberal sun
Shall move and shine without us, and we lie
Dead; but if she too move on earth and live,
But if the old world with all the old irons rent
Laugh and give thanks, shall we be not content?
Nay, we shall rather live, we shall not die,
Life being so little and death so good to give.

—And these men shall forget you.—Yea, but we
Shall be a part of the earth and the ancient sea,
And heaven-high air august, and awful fire,
And all things good; and no man's heart shall beat
But somewhat in it of our blood once shed
Shall quiver and quicken, as now in us the dead
Blood of men slain and the old same life's desire
Plants in their fiery footprints our fresh feet.

—But ye that might be clothed with all things pleasant,
Ye are foolish that put off the fair soft present,
That clothe yourselves with the cold future air;
When mother and father and tender sister and brother
And the old live love that was shall be as ye,
Dust, and no fruit of loving life shall be.
—She shall be yet who is more than all these were,
Than sister or wife or father unto us or mother.

—Is this worth life, is this, to win for wages?
Lo, the dead mouths of the awful grey-grown ages,
The venerable, in the past that is their prison,
In the outer darkness, in the unopening grave,
Laugh, knowing how many as ye now say have said,
How many, and all are fallen, are fallen and dead:
Shall ye dead rise, and these dead have not risen?
—Not we but she, who is tender and swift to save

—Are ye not weary and faint not by the way,
Seeing night by night devoured of day by day,

Seeing hour by hour consumed in sleepless fire?
Sleepless: and ye too, when shall ye too sleep?
—We are weary in heart and head, in hands and feet,
And surely more than all things sleep were sweet,
Than all things save the inexorable desire
Which whoso knoweth shall neither faint nor weep.

—Is this so sweet that one were fain to follow?
Is this so sure where all men's hopes are hollow,
Even this your dream, that by much tribulation
Ye shall make whole flawed hearts, and bowed necks straight?
—Nay, though our life were blind, our death were fruitless,
Not therefore were the whole world's high hope rootless;
But man to man, nation would turn to nation,
And the old life live, and the old great word be great.

—Pass on then and pass by us and let us be,
For what light think ye after life to see?
And if the world fare better will ye know?
And if man triumph who shall seek you and say?
—Enough of light is this for one life's span,
That all men born are mortal, but not man:
And we men bring death lives by night to sow,
That man may reap and eat and live by day.

ARMAND BARBÉS

I

Fire out of heaven, a flower of perfect fire,
That where the roots of life are had its root
And where the fruits of time are brought forth fruit;
A faith made flesh, a visible desire,
That heard the yet unbreathing years respire
And speech break forth of centuries that sit mute
Beyond all feebler footprint of pursuit;
That touched the highest of hope, and went up higher;
A heart love-wounded whereto love was law,
A soul reproachless without fear or flaw,
A shining spirit without shadow of shame,
A memory made of all men's love and awe;
Being disembodied, so thou be the same,
What need, O soul, to sign thee with thy name?

II

All woes of all men sat upon thy soul
And all their wrongs were heavy on thy head;
With all their wounds thy heart was pierced and bled,
And in thy spirit as in a mourning scroll
The world's huge sorrows were inscribed by roll,
All theirs on earth who serve and faint for bread,
All banished men's, all theirs in prison dead,
Thy love had heart and sword-hand for the whole.
"This was my day of glory," didst thou say,
When, by the scaffold thou hadst hope to climb
For thy faith's sake, they brought thee respite; "Nay,
I shall not die then, I have missed my day."
O hero, O our help, O head sublime,
Thy day shall be commensurate with time.

QUIA MULTUM AMAVIT

Am I not he that hath made thee and begotten thee,
I, God, the spirit of man?
Wherefore now these eighteen years hast thou forgotten me,
From whom thy life began?
Thy life-blood and thy life-breath and thy beauty,
Thy might of hands and feet,
Thy soul made strong for divinity of duty
And service which was sweet.
Through the red sea brimmed with blood didst thou not follow me,
As one that walks in trance?
Was the storm strong to break or the sea to swallow thee,
When thou wast free and France?
I am Freedom, God and man, O France, that plead with thee;
How long now shall I plead?
Was I not with thee in travail, and in need with thee,
Thy sore travail and need?
Thou wast fairest and first of my virgin-vested daughters,
Fairest and foremost thou;
And thy breast was white, though thy hands were red with slaughters,
Thy breast, a harlot's now.
O foolish virgin and fair among the fallen,
A ruin where satyrs dance,
A garden wasted for beasts to crawl and brawl in,
What hast thou done with France?
Where is she who bared her bosom but to thunder,
Her brow to storm and flame,
And before her face was the red sea cloven in sunder
And all its waves made tame?

And the surf wherein the broad-based rocks were shaking
She saw far off divide,
At the blast of the breath of the battle blown and breaking,
And weight of wind and tide;
And the ravin and the ruin of throned nations
And every royal race,
And the kingdoms and kings from the state of their high stations
That fell before her face.
Yea, great was the fall of them, all that rose against her,
From the earth's old-historied heights;
For my hands were fire, and my wings as walls that fenced her,
Mine eyes as pilot-lights.
Not as guerdons given of kings the gifts I brought her,
Not strengths that pass away;
But my heart, my breath of life, O France, O daughter,
I gave thee in that day.
Yea, the heart's blood of a very God I gave thee,
Breathed in thy mouth his breath;
Was my word as a man's, having no more strength to save thee
From this worse thing than death?
Didst thou dream of it only, the day that I stood nigh thee,
Was all its light a dream?
When that iron surf roared backwards and went by thee
Unscathed of storm or stream:
When thy sons rose up and thy young men stood together,
One equal face of fight,
And my flag swam high as the swimming sea-foam's feather,
Laughing, a lamp of light?
Ah the lordly laughter and light of it, that lightened
Heaven-high, the heaven's whole length!
Ah the hearts of heroes pierced, the bright lips whitened
Of strong men in their strength!
Ah the banner-poles, the stretch of straightening streamers
Straining their full reach out!
Ah the men's hands making true the dreams of dreamers,
The hopes brought forth in doubt!
Ah the noise of horse, the charge and thunder of drumming,
And swaying and sweep of swords!
Ah the light that led them through of the world's life coming,
Clear of its lies and lords!
By the lightning of the lips of guns whose flashes
Made plain the strayed world's way;
By the flame that left her dead old sins in ashes,
Swept out of sight of day;
By thy children whose bare feet were shod with thunder,
Their bare hands mailed with fire;
By the faith that went with them, waking fear and wonder,
Heart's love and high desire;

By the tumult of the waves of nations waking
Blind in the loud wide night;
By the wind that went on the world's waste waters, making
Their marble darkness white,
As the flash of the flakes of the foam flared lamplike, leaping
From wave to gladdening wave,
Making wide the fast-shut eyes of thraldom sleeping
The sleep of the unclean grave;
By the fire of equality, terrible, devouring,
Divine, that brought forth good;
By the lands it purged and wasted and left flowering
With bloom of brotherhood;
By the lips of fraternity that for love's sake uttered
Fierce words and fires of death,
But the eyes were deep as love's, and the fierce lips fluttered
With love's own living breath;
By thy weaponed hands, brows helmed, and bare feet spurning
The bared head of a king;
By the storm of sunrise round thee risen and burning,
Why hast thou done this thing?
Thou hast mixed thy limbs with the son of a harlot, a stranger,
Mouth to mouth, limb to limb,
Thou, bride of a God, because of the bridesman Danger,
To bring forth seed to him.
For thou thoughtest inly, the terrible bridegroom wakes me,
When I would sleep, to go;
The fire of his mouth consumes, and the red kiss shakes me,
More bitter than a blow.
Rise up, my beloved, go forth to meet the stranger,
Put forth thine arm, he saith;
Fear thou not at all though the bridesman should be Danger,
The bridesmaid should be Death.
I the bridegroom, am I not with thee, O bridal nation,
O wedded France, to strive?
To destroy the sins of the earth with divine devastation,
Till none be left alive?
Lo her growths of sons, foliage of men and frondage,
Broad boughs of the old-world tree,
With iron of shame and with pruning-hooks of bondage
They are shorn from sea to sea.
Lo, I set wings to thy feet that have been wingless,
Till the utter race be run;
Till the priestless temples cry to the thrones made kingless,
Are we not also undone?
Till the immeasurable Republic arise and lighten
Above these quick and dead,
And her awful robes be changed, and her red robes whiten,
Her warring-robes of red.

But thou wouldst not, saying, I am weary and faint to follow,
Let me lie down and rest;
And hast sought out shame to sleep with, mire to wallow,
Yea, a much fouler breast:
And thine own hast made prostitute, sold and shamed and bared it,
Thy bosom which was mine,
And the bread of the word I gave thee hast soiled, and shared it
Among these snakes and swine.
As a harlot thou wast handled and polluted,
Thy faith held light as foam,
That thou sentest men thy sons, thy sons imbruted,
To slay thine elder Rome.
Therefore O harlot, I gave thee to the accurst one,
By night to be defiled,
To thy second shame, and a fouler than the first one,
That got thee first with child.
Yet I know thee turning back now to behold me,
To bow thee and make thee bare,
Not for sin's sake but penitence, by my feet to hold me,
And wipe them with thine hair.
And sweet ointment of thy grief thou hast brought thy master,
And set before thy lord,
From a box of flawed and broken alabaster,
Thy broken spirit, poured.
And love-offerings, tears and perfumes, hast thou given me,
To reach my feet and touch;
Therefore thy sins, which are many, are forgiven thee,
Because thou hast loved much.

GENESIS

In the outer world that was before this earth,
That was before all shape or space was born,
Before the blind first hour of time had birth,
Before night knew the moonlight or the morn;
Yea, before any world had any light,
Or anything called God or man drew breath,
Slowly the strong sides of the heaving night
Moved, and brought forth the strength of life and death.

And the sad shapeless horror increate
That was all things and one thing, without fruit,
Limit, or law; where love was none, nor hate,
Where no leaf came to blossom from no root;

The very darkness that time knew not of,

Nor God laid hand on, nor was man found there,
Ceased, and was cloven in several shapes; above
Light, and night under, and fire, earth, water, and air.

Sunbeams and starbeams, and all coloured things,
All forms and all similitudes began;
And death, the shadow cast by life's wide wings,
And God, the shade cast by the soul of man.

Then between shadow and substance, night and light,
Then between birth and death, and deeds and days,
The illimitable embrace and the amorous fight
That of itself begets, bears, rears, and slays,

The immortal war of mortal things that is
Labour and life and growth and good and ill,
The mild antiphonies that melt and kiss,
The violent symphonies that meet and kill,

All nature of all things began to be.
But chiefliest in the spirit (beast or man,
Planet of heaven or blossom of earth or sea)
The divine contraries of life began.

For the great labour of growth, being many, is one;
One thing the white death and the ruddy birth;
The invisible air and the all-beholden sun,
And barren water and many-childed earth.

And these things are made manifest in men
From the beginning forth unto this day:
Time writes and life records them, and again
Death seals them lest the record pass away.

For if death were not, then should growth not be,
Change, nor the life of good nor evil things;
Nor were there night at all nor light to see,
Nor water of sweet nor water of bitter springs.

For in each man and each year that is born
Are sown the twin seeds of the strong twin powers;
The white seed of the fruitful helpful morn,
The black seed of the barren hurtful hours.

And he that of the black seed eateth fruit,
To him the savour as honey shall be sweet;
And he in whom the white seed hath struck root,
He shall have sorrow and trouble and tears for meat.

And him whose lips the sweet fruit hath made red
In the end men loathe and make his name a rod;
And him whose mouth on the unsweet fruit hath fed
In the end men follow and know for very God.

And of these twain, the black seed and the white,
All things come forth, endured of men and done;
And still the day is great with child of night,
And still the black night labours with the sun.

And each man and each year that lives on earth
Turns hither or thither, and hence or thence is fed;
And as a man before was from his birth,
So shall a man be after among the dead.

TO WALT WHITMAN IN AMERICA

Send but a song oversea for us,
Heart of their hearts who are free,
Heart of their singer, to be for us
More than our singing can be;
Ours, in the tempest at error,
With no light but the twilight of terror;
Send us a song oversea!
Sweet-smelling of pine-leaves and grasses,
And blown as a tree through and through
With the winds of the keen mountain-passes,
And tender as sun-smitten dew;
Sharp-tongued as the winter that shakes
The wastes of your limitless lakes,
Wide-eyed as the sea-line's blue.

O strong-winged soul with prophetic
Lips hot with the bloodheats of song,
With tremor of heartstrings magnetic,
With thoughts as thunders in throng,
With consonant ardours of chords
That pierce men's souls as with swords
And hale them hearing along,

Make us too music, to be with us
As a word from a world's heart warm,
To sail the dark as a sea with us,
Full-sailed, outsinging the storm,
A song to put fire in our ears

Whose burning shall burn up tears,
Whose sign bid battle reform;

A note in the ranks of a clarion,
A word in the wind of cheer,
To consume as with lightning the carrion
That makes time foul for us here;
In the air that our dead things infest
A blast of the breath of the west,
Till east way as west way is clear.

Out of the sun beyond sunset,
From the evening whence morning shall be,
With the rollers in measureless onset,
With the van of the storming sea,
With the world-wide wind, with the breath
That breaks ships driven upon death,
With the passion of all things free,

With the sea-steeds footless and frantic,
White myriads for death to bestride
In the charge of the ruining Atlantic
Where deaths by regiments ride,
With clouds and clamours of waters,
With a long note shriller than slaughter's
On the furrowless fields world-wide,

With terror, with ardour and wonder,
With the soul of the season that wakes
When the weight of a whole year's thunder
In the tidestream of autumn breaks,
Let the flight of the wide-winged word
Come over, come in and be heard,
Take form and fire for our sakes.

For a continent bloodless with travail
Here toils and brawls as it can,
And the web of it who shall unravel
Of all that peer on the plan;
Would fain grow men, but they grow not,
And fain be free, but they know not
One name for freedom and man?

One name, not twain for division;
One thing, not twain, from the birth;
Spirit and substance and vision,
Worth more than worship is worth;
Unbeheld, unadored, undivined,

The cause, the centre, the mind,
The secret and sense of the earth.

Here as a weakling in irons,
Here as a weanling in bands,
As a prey that the stake-net environs,
Our life that we looked for stands;
And the man-child naked and dear,
Democracy, turns on us here
Eyes trembling with tremulous hands

It sees not what season shall bring to it
Sweet fruit of its bitter desire;
Few voices it hears yet sing to it,
Few pulses of hearts reaspire;
Foresees not time, nor forehears
The noises of imminent years,
Earthquake, and thunder, and fire:

When crowned and weaponed and curbless
It shall walk without helm or shield
The bare burnt furrows and herbless
Of war's last flame-stricken field,
Till godlike, equal with time,
It stand in the sun sublime,
In the godhead of man revealed.

Round your people and over them
Light like raiment is drawn,
Close as a garment to cover them
Wrought not of mail nor of lawn;
Here, with hope hardly to wear,
Naked nations and bare
Swim, sink, strike out for the dawn.

Chains are here, and a prison,
Kings, and subjects, and shame;
If the God upon you be arisen,
How should our songs be the same?
How, in confusion of change,
How shall we sing, in a strange
Land, songs praising his name?

God is buried and dead to us,
Even the spirit of earth,
Freedom; so have they said to us,
Some with mocking and mirth,
Some with heartbreak and tears;

And a God without eyes, without ears,
Who shall sing of him, dead in the birth?

The earth-god Freedom, the lonely
Face lightening, the footprint unshod,
Not as one man crucified only
Nor scourged with but one life's rod;
The soul that is substance of nations,
Reincarnate with fresh generations;
The great god Man, which is God.

But in weariest of years and obscurest
Doth it live not at heart of all things,
The one God and one spirit, a purest
Life, fed from unstanchable springs?
Within love, within hatred it is,
And its seed in the stripe as the kiss,
And in slaves is the germ, and in kings.

Freedom we call it, for holier
Name of the soul's there is none;
Surelier it labours if slowlier,
Than the metres of star or of sun;
Slowlier than life into breath,
Surelier than time into death,
It moves till its labour be done.

Till the motion be done and the measure
Circling through season and clime,
Slumber and sorrow and pleasure,
Vision of virtue and crime;
Till consummate with conquering eyes,
A soul disembodied, it rise
From the body transfigured of time.

Till it rise and remain and take station
With the stars of the worlds that rejoice;
Till the voice of its heart's exultation
Be as theirs an invariable voice;
By no discord of evil estranged,
By no pause, by no breach in it changed,
By no clash in the chord of its choice.

It is one with the world's generations,
With the spirit, the star, and the sod;
With the kingless and king-stricken nations,
With the cross, and the chain, and the rod;
The most high, the most secret, most lonely,

The earth-soul Freedom, that only
Lives, and that only is God.

I

IN CHURCH

Thou whose birth on earth
Angels sang to men,
While thy stars made mirth,
Saviour, at thy birth,
This day born again;

As this night was bright
With thy cradle-ray,
Very light of light,
Turn the wild world's night
To thy perfect day.

God whose feet made sweet
Those wild ways they trod,
From thy fragrant feet
Staining field and street
With the blood of God;

God whose breast is rest
In the time of strife,
In thy secret breast
Sheltering souls opprest
From the heat of life;

God whose eyes are skies
Love-lit as with spheres
By the lights that rise
To thy watching eyes,
Orbed lights of tears;

God whose heart hath part
In all grief that is,
Was not man's the dart
That went through thine heart,
And the wound not his?

Where the pale souls wail,

Held in bonds of death,
Where all spirits quail,
Came thy Godhead pale
Still from human breath—

Pale from life and strife,
Wan with manhood, came
Forth of mortal life,
Pierced as with a knife,
Scarred as with a flame.

Thou the Word and Lord
In all time and space
Heard, beheld, adored,
With all ages poured
Forth before thy face,

Lord, what worth in earth
Drew thee down to die?
What therein was worth,
Lord, thy death and birth?
What beneath thy sky?

Light above all love
By thy love was lit,
And brought down the Dove
Feathered from above
With the wings of it.

From the height of night,
Was not thine the star
That led forth with might
By no worldly light
Wise men from afar?

Yet the wise men's eyes
Saw thee not more clear
Than they saw thee rise
Who in shepherd's guise
Drew as poor men near.

Yet thy poor endure,
And are with us yet;
Be thy name a sure
Refuge for thy poor
Whom men's eyes forget.

Thou whose ways we praised,

Clear alike and dark,
Keep our works and ways
This and all thy days
Safe inside thine ark.

Who shall keep thy sheep,
Lord, and lose not one?
Who save one shall keep,
Lest the shepherds sleep?
Who beside the Son?

From the grave-deep wave,
From the sword and flame,
Thou, even thou, shalt save
Souls of king and slave
Only by thy Name.

Light not born with morn
Or her fires above,
Jesus virgin-born,
Held of men in scorn,
Turn their scorn to love.

Thou whose face gives grace
As the sun's doth heat,
Let thy sunbright face
Lighten time and space
Here beneath thy feet.

Bid our peace increase,
Thou that madest morn;
Bid oppressions cease;
Bid the night be peace;
Bid the day be born.

II

OUTSIDE CHURCH

We whose days and ways
All the night makes dark,
What day shall we praise
Of these weary days
That our life-drops mark?

We whose mind is blind,
Fed with hope of nought;

Wastes of worn mankind,
Without heart or mind,
Without meat or thought;

We with strife of life
Worn till all life cease,
Want, a whetted knife,
Sharpening strife on strife,
How should we love peace?

Ye whose meat is sweet
And your wine-cup red,
Us beneath your feet
Hunger grinds as wheat,
Grinds to make you bread.

Ye whose night is bright
With soft rest and heat,
Clothed like day with light,
Us the naked night
Slays from street to street.

Hath your God no rod,
That ye tread so light?
Man on us as God,
God as man hath trod,
Trod us down with might.

We that one by one
Bleed from either's rod.
What for us hath done
Man beneath the sun,
What for us hath God?

We whose blood is food
Given your wealth to feed,
From the Christless rood
Red with no God's blood,
But with man's indeed;

How shall we that see
Nightlong overhead
Life, the flowerless tree,
Nailed whereon as we
Were our fathers dead—

We whose ear can hear,
Not whose tongue can name,

Famine, ignorance, fear,
Bleeding tear by tear
Year by year of shame,

Till the dry life die
Out of bloodless breast,
Out of beamless eye,
Out of mouths that cry
Till death feed with rest—

How shall we as ye,
Though ye bid us, pray?
Though ye call, can we
Hear you call, or see,
Though ye show us day?

We whose name is shame,
We whose souls walk bare,
Shall we call the same
God as ye by name,
Teach our lips your prayer?

God, forgive and give,
For His sake who died?
Nay, for ours who live,
How shall we forgive
Thee, then, on our side?

We whose right to light
Heaven's high noon denies,
Whom the blind beams smite
That for you shine bright,
And but burn our eyes,

With what dreams of beams
Shall we build up day,
At what sourceless streams
Seek to drink in dreams
Ere they pass away?

In what street shall meet,
At what market-place,
Your feet and our feet,
With one goal to greet,
Having run one race?

What one hope shall ope
For us all as one

One same horoscope,
Where the soul sees hope
That outburns the sun?

At what shrine what wine,
At what board what bread,
Salt as blood or brine,
Shall we share in sign
How we poor were fed?

In what hour what power
Shall we pray for morn,
If your perfect hour,
When all day bears flower,
Not for us is born?

III

BEYOND CHURCH

Ye that weep in sleep,
Souls and bodies bound,
Ye that all night keep
Watch for change, and weep
That no change is found;

Ye that cry and die,
And the world goes on
Without ear or eye,
And the days go by
Till all days are gone;

Man shall do for you,
Men the sons of man,
What no God would do
That they sought unto
While the blind years ran.

Brotherhood of good,
Equal laws and rights,
Freedom, whose sweet food
Feeds the multitude
All their days and nights

With the bread full-fed
Of her body blest
And the soul's wine shed

From her table spread
Where the world is guest,

Mingling me and thee,
When like light of eyes
Flashed through thee and me
Truth shall make us free,
Liberty make wise;

These are they whom day
Follows and gives light
Whence they see to slay
Night, and burn away
All the seed of night.

What of thine and mine,
What of want and wealth,
When one faith is wine
For my heart and thine
And one draught is health?

For no sect elect
Is the soul's wine poured
And her table decked;
Whom should man reject
From man's common board?

Gods refuse and choose,
Grudge and sell and spare;
None shall man refuse,
None of all men lose,
None leave out of care.

No man's might of sight
Knows that hour before;
No man's hand hath might
To put back that light
For one hour the more.

Not though all men call,
Kneeling with void hands,
Shall they see light fall
Till it come for all
Tribes of men and lands.

No desire brings fire
Down from heaven by prayer,
Though man's vain desire

Hang faith's wind-struck lyre
Out in tuneless air.

One hath breath and saith
What the tune shall be—
Time, who puts his breath
Into life and death,
Into earth and sea.

To and fro years flow,
Fill their tides and ebb,
As his fingers go
Weaving to and fro
One unfinished web.

All the range of change
Hath its bounds therein,
All the lives that range
All the byways strange
Named of death or sin.

Star from far to star
Speaks, and white moons wake,
Watchful from afar
What the night's ways are
For the morning's sake.

Many names and flames
Pass and flash and fall,
Night-begotten names,
And the night reclaims,
As she bare them, all.

But the sun is one,
And the sun's name Right;
And when light is none
Saving of the sun,
All men shall have light.

All shall see and be
Parcel of the morn;
Ay, though blind were we,
None shall choose but see
When that day is born.

A NEW YEAR'S MESSAGE

To Joseph Mazzini

Send the stars light, but send not love to me.
SHELLEY.

I

Out of the dawning heavens that hear
Young wings and feet of the new year
Move through their twilight, and shed round
Soft showers of sound,
Soothing the season with sweet rain,
If greeting come to make me fain,
What is it I can send again?

II

I know not if the year shall send
Tidings to usward as a friend,
And salutation, and such things
Bear on his wings
As the soul turns and thirsts unto
With hungering eyes and lips that sue
For that sweet food which makes all new.

III

I know not if his light shall be
Darkness, or else light verily:
I know but that it will not part
Heart's faith from heart,
Truth from the trust in truth, nor hope
From sight of days unscaled that ope
Beyond one poor year's horoscope.

IV

That faith in love which love's self gives,
O master of my spirit, lives,
Having in presence unremoved
Thine head beloved,
The shadow of thee, the semitone
Of thy voice heard at heart and known,
The light of thee not set nor flown.

V

Seas, lands, and hours, can these divide
Love from love's service, side from side,
Though no sound pass nor breath be heard
Of one good word?
To send back words of trust to thee
Were to send wings to love, when he
With his own strong wings covers me.

VI

Who shall teach singing to the spheres,
Or motion to the flight of years?
Let soul with soul keep hand in hand
And understand,
As in one same abiding-place
We keep one watch for one same face
To rise in some short sacred space.

VII

And all space midway is but nought
To keep true heart from faithful thought,
As under twilight stars we wait
By Time's shut gate
Till the slow soundless hinges turn,
And through the depth of years that yearn
The face of the Republic burn.

1870.

MASTER DOLOROSA

Citoyen, lui dit Enjoiras, ma mère, c'est la République.
Les Misérables.

Who is this that sits by the way, by the wild wayside,
In a rent stained raiment, the robe of a cast-off bride,
In the dust, in the rainfall sitting, with soiled feet bare,
With the night for a garment upon her, with torn wet hair?
She is fairer of face than the daughters of men, and her eyes,
Worn through with her tears, are deep as the depth of skies.

This is she for whose sake being fallen, for whose abject sake,
Earth groans in the blackness of darkness, and men's hearts break.
This is she for whose love, having seen her, the men that were
Poured life out as water, and shed their souls upon air.
This is she for whose glory their years were counted as foam;
Whose face was a light upon Greece, was a fire upon Rome.

Is it now not surely a vain thing, a foolish and vain,
To sit down by her, mourn to her, serve her, partake in the pain?
She is grey with the dust of time on his manifold ways,
Where her faint feet stumble and falter through year-long days.
Shall she help us at all, O fools, give fruit or give fame,
Who herself is a name despised, a rejected name?

We have not served her for guerdon. If any do so,
That his mouth may be sweet with such honey, we care not to know.
We have drunk from a wine-unsweetened, a perilous cup,
A draught very bitter. The kings of the earth stood up,
And the rulers took counsel together, to smite her and slay;
And the blood of her wounds is given us to drink today.

Can these bones live? or the leaves that are dead leaves bud?
Or the dead blood drawn from her veins be in your veins blood?
Will ye gather up water again that was drawn and shed?
In the blood is the life of the veins, and her veins are dead.
For the lives that are over are over, and past things past;
She had her day, and it is not; was first, and is last.

Is it nothing unto you then, all ye that pass by,
If her breath be left in her lips, if she live now or die?
Behold now, O people, and say if she be not fair,
Whom your fathers followed to find her, with praise and prayer,
And rejoiced, having found her, though roof they had none nor bread;
But ye care not; what is it to you if her day be dead?

It was well with our fathers; their sound was in all men's lands;
There was fire in their hearts, and the hunger of fight in their hands.
Naked and strong they went forth in her strength like flame,
For her love's and her name's sake of old, her republican name.
But their children, by kings made quiet, by priests made wise,
Love better the heat of their hearths than the light of her eyes.

Are they children of these thy children indeed, who have sold,
O golden goddess, the light of thy face for gold?
Are they sons indeed of the sons of thy dayspring of hope,
Whose lives are in fief of an emperor, whose souls of a Pope?
Hide then thine head, O beloved; thy time is done;
Thy kingdom is broken in heaven, and blind thy sun.

What sleep is upon you, to dream she indeed shall rise,
When the hopes are dead in her heart as the tears in her eyes?
If ye sing of her dead, will she stir? if ye weep for her, weep?
Come away now, leave her; what hath she to do but sleep?
But ye that mourn are alive, and have years to be;
And life is good, and the world is wiser than we.

Yea, wise is the world and mighty, with years to give,
And years to promise; but how long now shall it live?
And foolish and poor is faith, and her ways are bare,
Till she find the way of the sun, and the morning air.
In that hour shall this dead face shine as the face of the sun,
And the soul of man and her soul and the world's be one.

MATER TRIUMPHALIS

Mother of man's time-travelling generations,
Breath of his nostrils, heartblood of his heart,
God above all Gods worshipped of all nations,
Light above light, law beyond law, thou art.
Thy face is as a sword smiting in sunder
Shadows and chains and dreams and iron things;
The sea is dumb before thy face, the thunder
Silent, the skies are narrower than thy wings.

Angels and Gods, spirit and sense, thou takest
In thy right hand as drops of dust or dew;
The temples and the towers of time thou breakest,
His thoughts and words and works, to make them new.

All we have wandered from thy ways, have hidden
Eyes from thy glory and ears from calls they heard;
Called of thy trumpets vainly, called and chidden,
Scourged of thy speech and wounded of thy word.

We have known thee and have not known thee; stood beside thee,
Felt thy lips breathe, set foot where thy feet trod,
Loved and renounced and worshipped and denied thee,
As though thou wert but as another God,

"One hour for sleep," we said, "and yet one other;
All day we served her, and who shall serve by night?"
Not knowing of thee, thy face not knowing, O mother,
O light wherethrough the darkness is as light.

Men that forsook thee hast thou not forsaken,
Races of men that knew not hast thou known;
Nations that slept thou hast doubted not to waken,
Worshippers of strange Gods to make thine own.

All old grey histories hiding thy clear features,
O secret spirit and sovereign, all men's tales,
Creeds woven of men thy children and thy creatures,
They have woven for vestures of thee and for veils.

Thine hands, without election or exemption,
Feed all men fainting from false peace or strife,
O thou, the resurrection and redemption,
The godhead and the manhood and the life.

Thy wings shadow the waters; thine eyes lighten
The horror of the hollows of the night;
The depths of the earth and the dark places brighten
Under thy feet, whiter than fire is white.

Death is subdued to thee, and hell's bands broken;
Where thou art only is heaven; who hears not thee,
Time shall not hear him; when men's names are spoken,
A nameless sign of death shall his name be.

Deathless shall be the death, the name be nameless;
Sterile of stars his twilight time of breath;
With fire of hell shall shame consume him shameless,
And dying, all the night darken his death.

The years are as thy garments, the world's ages
As sandals bound and loosed from thy swift feet;
Time serves before thee, as one that hath for wages
Praise or shame only, bitter words or sweet.

Thou sayest "Well done," and all a century kindles;
Again thou sayest "Depart from sight of me,"
And all the light of face of all men dwindles,
And the age is as the broken glass of thee.

The night is as a seal set on men's faces,
On faces fallen of men that take no light,
Nor give light in the deeps of the dark places,
Blind things, incorporate with the body of night.

Their souls are serpents winterbound and frozen,
Their shame is as a tame beast, at their feet
Couched; their cold lips deride thee and thy chosen,

Their lying lips made grey with dust for meat.

Then when their time is full and days run over,
The splendour of thy sudden brow made bare
Darkens the morning; thy bared hands uncover
The veils of light and night and the awful air.

And the world naked as a new-born maiden
Stands virginal and splendid as at birth,
With all thine heaven of all its light unladen,
Of all its love unburdened all thine earth.

For the utter earth and the utter air of heaven
And the extreme depth is thine and the extreme height;
Shadows of things and veils of ages riven
Are as men's kings unkingdomed in thy sight.

Through the iron years, the centuries brazen-gated,
By the ages' barred impenetrable doors,
From the evening to the morning have we waited,
Should thy foot haply sound on the awful floors.

The floors untrodden of the sun's feet glimmer,
The star-unstricken pavements of the night;
Do the lights burn inside? the lights wax dimmer
On festal faces withering out of sight.

The crowned heads lose the light on them; it may be
Dawn is at hand to smite the loud feast dumb;
To blind the torch-lit centuries till the day be,
The feasting kingdoms till thy kingdom come.

Shall it not come? deny they or dissemble,
Is it not even as lightning from on high
Now? and though many a soul close eyes and tremble,
How should they tremble at all who love thee as I?

I am thine harp between thine hands, O mother!
All my strong chords are strained with love of thee.
We grapple in love and wrestle, as each with other
Wrestle the wind and the unreluctant sea.

I am no courtier of thee sober-suited,
Who loves a little for a little pay.
Me not thy winds and storms nor thrones disrooted
Nor molten crowns nor thine own sins dismay.

Sinned hast thou sometime, therefore art thou sinless;

Stained hast thou been, who art therefore without stain;
Even as man's soul is kin to thee, but kinless
Thou, in whose womb Time sows the all-various grain.

I do not bid thee spare me, O dreadful mother!
I pray thee that thou spare not, of thy grace.
How were it with me then, if ever another
Should come to stand before thee in this my place?

I am the trumpet at thy lips, thy clarion
Full of thy cry, sonorous with thy breath;
The graves of souls born worms and creeds grown carrion
Thy blast of judgment fills with fires of death.

Thou art the player whose organ-keys are thunders,
And I beneath thy foot the pedal prest;
Thou art the ray whereat the rent night sunders,
And I the cloudlet borne upon thy breast.

I shall burn up before thee, pass and perish,
As haze in sunrise on the red sea-line;
But thou from dawn to sunsetting shalt cherish
The thoughts that led and souls that lighted mine.

Reared between night and noon and truth and error,
Each twilight-travelling bird that trills and screams
Sickens at midday, nor can face for terror
The imperious heaven's inevitable extremes.

I have no spirit of skill with equal fingers
At sign to sharpen or to slacken strings;
I keep no time of song with gold-perched singers
And chirp of linnets on the wrists of kings.

I am thy storm-thrush of the days that darken,
Thy petrel in the foam that bears thy bark
To port through night and tempest; if thou hearken,
My voice is in thy heaven before the lark.

My song is in the mist that hides thy morning,
My cry is up before the day for thee;
I have heard thee and beheld thee and give warning,
Before thy wheels divide the sky and sea.

Birds shall wake with thee voiced and feathered fairer,
To see in summer what I see in spring;
I have eyes and heart to endure thee, O thunder-bearer,
And they shall be who shall have tongues to sing.

I have love at least, and have not fear, and part not
From thine unnavigable and wingless way;
Thou tarriest, and I have not said thou art not,
Nor all thy night long have denied thy day.

Darkness to daylight shall lift up thy pæan,
Hill to hill thunder, vale cry back to vale,
With wind-notes as of eagles Æschylean,
And Sappho singing in the nightingale.

Sung to by mighty sons of dawn and daughters,
Of this night's songs thine ear shall keep but one;
That supreme song which shook the channelled waters,
And called thee skyward as God calls the sun.

Come, though all heaven again be fire above thee;
Though death before thee come to clear thy sky;
Let us but see in his thy face who love thee;
Yea, though thou slay us, arise and let us die.

A MARCHING SONG

We mix from many lands,
We march for very far;
In hearts and lips and hands
Our staffs and weapons are;
The light we walk in darkens sun and moon and star.
It doth not flame and wane
With years and spheres that roll,
Storm cannot shake nor stain
The strength that makes it whole,
The fire that moulds and moves it of the sovereign soul.

We are they that have to cope
With time till time retire;
We live on hopeless hope,
We feed on tears and fire;
Time, foot by foot, gives back before our sheer desire.

From the edge of harsh derision,
From discord and defeat,
From doubt and lame division,
We pluck the fruit and eat;
And the mouth finds it bitter, and the spirit sweet.

We strive with time at wrestling
Till time be on our side
And hope, our plumeless nestling,
A full-fledged eaglet ride
Down the loud length of storm its windward wings divide.

We are girt with our belief,
Clothed with our will and crowned;
Hope, fear, delight, and grief,
Before our will give ground;
Their calls are in our ears as shadows of dead sound.

All but the heart forsakes us,
All fails us but the will;
Keen treason tracks and takes us
In pits for blood to fill;
Friend falls from friend, and faith for faith lays wait to kill.

Out under moon and stars
And shafts of the urgent sun
Whose face on prison-bars
And mountain-heads is one,
Our march is everlasting till time's march be done.

Whither we know, and whence,
And dare not care wherethrough.
Desires that urge the sense,
Fears changing old with new,
Perils and pains beset the ways we press into;

Earth gives us thorns to tread,
And all her thorns are trod;
Through lands burnt black and red
We pass with feet unshod;
Whence we would be man shall not keep us, nor man's God.

Through the great desert beasts
Howl at our backs by night,
And thunder-forging priests
Blow their dead bale-fires bright,
And on their broken anvils beat out bolts for fight.

Inside their sacred smithies
Though hot the hammer rings,
Their steel links snap like withies,
Their chains like twisted strings,
Their surest fetters are as plighted words of kings.

O nations undivided,
O single people and free,
We dreamers, we derided,
We mad blind men that see,
We bear you witness ere ye come that ye shall be.

Ye sitting among tombs,
Ye standing round the gate,
Whom fire-mouthed war consumes,
Or cold-lipped peace bids wait,
All tombs and bars shall open, every grave and grate.

The locks shall burst in sunder,
The hinges shrieking spin,
When time, whose hand is thunder,
Lays hand upon the pin,
And shoots the bolts reluctant, bidding all men in.

These eyeless times and earless,
Shall these not see and hear,
And all their hearts burn fearless
That were afrost for fear?
Is day not hard upon us, yea, not our day near?

France! from its grey dejection
Make manifest the red
Tempestuous resurrection
Of thy most sacred head!
Break thou the covering cerecloths; rise up from the dead.

And thou, whom sea-walls sever
From lands unwalled with seas,
Wilt thou endure for ever,
O Milton's England, these?
Thou that wast his Republic, wilt thou clasp their knees?

These royalties rust-eaten,
These worm-corroded lies,
That keep thine head storm-beaten
And sunlike strength of eyes
From the open heaven and air of intercepted skies;

These princelings with gauze winglets
That buzz in the air unfurled,
These summer-swarming kinglets,
These thin worms crowned and curled,
That bask and blink and warm themselves about the world;

These fanged meridian vermin,
Shrill gnats that crowd the dusk,
Night-moths whose nestling ermine
Smells foul of mould and musk,
Blind flesh-flies hatched by dark and hampered in their husk;

These honours without honour,
These ghost-like gods of gold,
This earth that wears upon her
To keep her heart from cold
No memory more of men that brought it fire of old;

These limbs, supine, unbuckled,
In rottenness of rest,
These sleepy lips blood-suckled
And satiate of thy breast,
These dull wide mouths that drain thee dry and call thee blest;

These masters of thee mindless
That wear thee out of mind,
These children of thee kindless
That use thee out of kind,
Whose hands strew gold before thee and contempt behind;

Who have turned thy name to laughter,
Thy sea-like sounded name
That now none hearkens after
For faith in its free fame,
Who have robbed thee of thy trust and given thee of their shame;

These hours that mock each other,
These years that kill and die,
Are these thy gains, our mother,
For all thy gains thrown by?
Is this that end whose promise made thine heart so high?

With empire and with treason
The first right hand made fast,
But in man's nobler season
To put forth help the last,
Love turns from thee, and memory disavows thy past.

Lest thine own sea disclaim thee,
Lest thine own sons despise,
Lest lips shoot out that name thee
And seeing thee men shut eyes,
Take thought with all thy people, turn thine head and rise.

Turn thee, lift up thy face;
What ails thee to be dead?
Ask of thyself for grace,
Seek of thyself for bread,
And who shall starve or shame thee, blind or bruise thine head?

The same sun in thy sight,
The same sea in thine ears,
That saw thine hour at height,
That sang thy song of years,
Behold and hearken for thee, knowing thy hopes and fears.

O people, O perfect nation,
O England that shall be,
How long till thou take station?
How long till thralls live free?
How long till all thy soul be one with all thy sea?

Ye that from south to north,
Ye that from east to west,
Stretch hands of longing forth
And keep your eyes from rest,
Lo, when ye will, we bring you gifts of what is best.

From the awful northland pines
That skirt their wan dim seas
To the ardent Apennines
And sun-struck Pyrenees,
One frost on all their frondage bites the blossoming trees.

The leaves look up for light,
For heat of helpful air;
The trees of oldest height
And thin storm-shaken hair
Seek with gaunt hands up heavenward if the sun be there.

The woods where souls walk lonely,
The forests girt with night,
Desire the day-star only
And firstlings of the light
Not seen of slaves nor shining in their masters' sight.

We have the morning star,
O foolish people, O kings!
With us the day-springs are,
Even all the fresh day-springs;
For us, and with us, all the multitudes of things.

O sorrowing hearts of slaves,
We heard you beat from far!
We bring the light that saves,
We bring the morning star;
Freedom's good things we bring you, whence all good things are.

With us the winds and fountains
And lightnings live in tune;
The morning-coloured mountains
That burn into the noon,
The mist's mild veil on valleys muffled from the moon:

The thunder-darkened highlands
And lowlands hot with fruit,
Sea-bays and shoals and islands,
And cliffs that foil man's foot,
And all the flower of large-limbed life and all the root:

The clangour of sea-eagles
That teach the morning mirth
With baying of heaven's beagles
That seek their prey on earth,
By sounding strait and channel, gulf and reach and firth.

With us the fields and rivers,
The grass that summer thrills,
The haze where morning quivers,
The peace at heart of hills,
The sense that kindles nature, and the soul that fills.

With us all natural sights,
All notes of natural scale;
With us the starry lights;
With us the nightingale;
With us the heart and secret of the worldly tale.

The strife of things and beauty,
The fire and light adored,
Truth, and life-lightening duty,
Love without crown or sword,
That by his might and godhead makes man god and lord.

These have we, these are ours,
That no priests give nor kings;
The honey of all these flowers,
The heart of all these springs;
Ours, for where freedom lives not, there live no good things.

Rise, ere the dawn be risen;
Come, and be all souls fed;
From field and street and prison
Come, for the feast is spread;
Live, for the truth is living; wake, for night is dead.

SIENA

Inside this northern summer's fold
The fields are full of naked gold,
Broadcast from heaven on lands it loves;
The green veiled air is full of doves;
Soft leaves that sift the sunbeams let
Light on the small warm grasses wet
Fall in short broken kisses sweet,
And break again like waves that beat
Round the sun's feet.
But I, for all this English mirth
Of golden-shod and dancing days,
And the old green-girt sweet-hearted earth,
Desire what here no spells can raise.
Far hence, with holier heavens above,
The lovely city of my love
Bathes deep in the sun-satiate air
That flows round no fair thing more fair
Her beauty bare.

There the utter sky is holier, there
More pure the intense white height of air,
More clear men's eyes that mine would meet,
And the sweet springs of things more sweet.
There for this one warm note of doves
A clamour of a thousand loves
Storms the night's ear, the day's assails,
From the tempestuous nightingales,
And fills, and fails.

O gracious city well-beloved,
Italian, and a maiden crowned,
Siena, my feet are no more moved
Toward thy strange-shapen mountain-bound:
But my heart in me turns and moves,
O lady loveliest of my loves,
Toward thee, to lie before thy feet
And gaze from thy fair fountain-seat
Up the sheer street;

And the house midway hanging see
That saw Saint Catherine bodily,
Felt on its floors her sweet feet move,
And the live light of fiery love
Burn from her beautiful strange face,
As in the sanguine sacred place
Where in pure hands she took the head
Severed, and with pure lips still red
Kissed the lips dead.

For years through, sweetest of the saints,
In quiet without cease she wrought,
Till cries of men and fierce complaints
From outward moved her maiden thought;
And prayers she heard and sighs toward France,
"God, send us back deliverance,
Send back thy servant, lest we die!"
With an exceeding bitter cry
They smote the sky.

Then in her sacred saving hands
She took the sorrows of the lands,
With maiden palms she lifted up
The sick time's blood-embittered cup,
And in her virgin garment furled
The faint limbs of a wounded world.
Clothed with calm love and clear desire,
She went forth in her soul's attire,
A missive fire.

Across the might of men that strove
It shone, and over heads of kings;
And molten in red flames of love
Were swords and many monstrous things;
And shields were lowered, and snapt were spears,
And sweeter-tuned the clamorous years;
And faith came back, and peace, that were
Fled; for she bade, saying, "Thou, God's heir,
Hast thou no care?

"Lo, men lay waste thine heritage
Still, and much heathen people rage
Against thee, and devise vain things.
What comfort in the face of kings,
What counsel is there? Turn thine eyes
And thine heart from them in like wise;
Turn thee unto thine holy place

To help us that of God for grace
Require thy face.

"For who shall hear us if not thou
In a strange land? what doest thou there?
Thy sheep are spoiled, and the ploughers plough
Upon us; why hast thou no care
For all this, and beyond strange hills
Liest unregardful what snow chills
Thy foldless flock, or what rains beat?
Lo, in thine ears, before thy feet,
Thy lost sheep bleat.

"And strange men feed on faultless lives,
And there is blood, and men put knives,
Shepherd, unto the young lamb's throat;
And one hath eaten, and one smote,
And one had hunger and is fed
Full of the flesh of these, and red
With blood of these as who drinks wine
And God knoweth, who hath sent thee a sign,
If these were thine."

But the Pope's heart within him burned,
So that he rose up, seeing the sign,
And came among them; but she turned
Back to her daily way divine,
And fed her faith with silent things,
And lived her life with curbed white wings,
And mixed herself with heaven and died:
And now on the sheer city-side
Smiles like a bride.

You see her in the fresh clear gloom,
Where walls shut out the flame and bloom
Of full-breathed summer, and the roof
Keeps the keen ardent air aloof
And sweet weight of the violent sky:
There bodily beheld on high,
She seems as one hearing in tune
Heaven within heaven, at heaven's full noon,
In sacred swoon:

A solemn swoon of sense that aches
With imminent blind heat of heaven,
While all the wide-eyed spirit wakes,
Vigilant of the supreme Seven,
Whose choral flames in God's sight move,

Made unendurable with love,
That without wind or blast of breath
Compels all things through life and death
Whither God saith.

There on the dim side-chapel wall
Thy mighty touch memorial,
Razzi, raised up, for ages dead,
And fixed for us her heavenly head:
And, rent with plaited thorn and rod,
Bared the live likeness of her God
To men's eyes turning from strange lands,
Where, pale from thine immortal hands,
Christ wounded stands;

And the blood blots his holy hair
And white brows over hungering eyes
That plead against us, and the fair
Mute lips forlorn of words or sighs
In the great torment that bends down
His bruised head with the bloomless crown,
White as the unfruitful thorn-flower,
A God beheld in dreams that were
Beheld of her.

In vain on all these sins and years
Falls the sad blood, fall the slow tears;
In vain poured forth as watersprings,
Priests, on your altars, and ye, kings,
About your seats of sanguine gold;
Still your God, spat upon and sold,
Bleeds at your hands; but now is gone
All his flock from him saving one;
Judas alone.

Surely your race it was that he,
O men signed backward with his name,
Beholding in Gethsemane
Bled the red bitter sweat of shame,
Knowing how the word of Christian should
Mean to men evil and not good,
Seem to men shameful for your sake,
Whose lips, for all the prayers they make,
Man's blood must slake.

But blood nor tears ye love not, you
That my love leads my longing to,
Fair as the world's old faith of flowers,

O golden goddesses of ours!
From what Idalian rose-pleasance
Hath Aphrodite bidden glance
The lovelier lightnings of your feet?
From what sweet Paphian sward or seat
Led you more sweet?

O white three sisters, three as one,
With flowerlike arms for flowery bands
Your linked limbs glitter like the sun,
And time lies beaten at your hands.
Time and wild years and wars and men
Pass, and ye care not whence or when;
With calm lips over sweet for scorn,
Ye watch night pass, O children born
Of the old-world morn.

Ah, in this strange and shrineless place,
What doth a goddess, what a Grace,
Where no Greek worships her shrined limbs
With wreaths and Cytherean hymns?
Where no lute makes luxurious
The adoring airs in Amathus,
Till the maid, knowing her mother near,
Sobs with love, aching with sweet fear?
What do ye here?

For the outer land is sad, and wears
A raiment of a flaming fire;
And the fierce fruitless mountain stairs
Climb, yet seem wroth and loth to aspire,
Climb, and break, and are broken down,
And through their clefts and crests the town
Looks west and sees the dead sun lie,
In sanguine death that stains the sky
With angry dye.

And from the war-worn wastes without
In twilight, in the time of doubt,
One sound comes of one whisper, where
Moved with low motions of slow air
The great trees nigh the castle swing
In the sad coloured evening;
"Ricorditi di me, che son
La Pia"—that small sweet word alone
Is not yet gone.

"Ricorditi di me"—the sound

Sole out of deep dumb days remote
Across the fiery and fatal ground
Comes tender as a hurt bird's note
To where, a ghost with empty hands,
A woe-worn ghost, her palace stands
In the mid city, where the strong
Bells turn the sunset air to song,
And the towers throng.

With other face, with speech the same,
A mightier maiden's likeness came
Late among mourning men that slept,
A sacred ghost that went and wept,
White as the passion-wounded Lamb,
Saying, "Ah, remember me, that am
Italia." (From deep sea to sea
Earth heard, earth knew her, that this was she.)
"Ricorditi.

"Love made me of all things fairest thing,
And Hate unmade me; this knows he
Who with God's sacerdotal ring
Enringed mine hand, espousing me."
Yea, in thy myriad-mooded woe,
Yea, Mother, hast thou not said so?
Have not our hearts within us stirred,
O thou most holiest, at thy word?
Have we not heard?

As this dead tragic land that she
Found deadly, such was time to thee;
Years passed thee withering in the red
Maremma, years that deemed thee dead,
Ages that sorrowed or that scorned;
And all this while though all they mourned
Thou sawest the end of things unclean,
And the unborn that should see thee a queen.
Have we not seen?

The weary poet, thy sad son,
Upon thy soil, under thy skies,
Saw all Italian things save one—
Italia; this thing missed his eyes;
The old mother-might, the breast, the face,
That reared, that lit the Roman race;
This not Leopardi saw; but we,
What is it, Mother, that we see,
What if not thee?

Look thou from Siena southward home,
Where the priest's pall hangs rent on Rome,
And through the red rent swaddling-bands
Towards thine she strains her labouring hands.
Look thou and listen, and let be
All the dead quick, all the bond free;
In the blind eyes let there be sight;
In the eighteen centuries of the night
Let there be light.

Bow down the beauty of thine head,
Sweet, and with lips of living breath
Kiss thy sons sleeping and thy dead,
That there be no more sleep or death.
Give us thy light, thy might, thy love,
Whom thy face seen afar above
Drew to thy feet; and when, being free,
Thou hast blest thy children born to thee,
Bless also me.

Me that when others played or slept
Sat still under thy cross and wept;
Me who so early and unaware
Felt fall on bent bared brows and hair
(Thin drops of the overflowing flood!)
The bitter blessing of thy blood;
The sacred shadow of thy pain,
Thine, the true maiden-mother, slain
And raised again.

Me consecrated, if I might,
To praise thee, or to love at least,
O mother of all men's dear delight,
Thou madest a choral-souled boy-priest,
Before my lips had leave to sing,
Or my hands hardly strength to cling
About the intolerable tree
Whereto they had nailed my heart and thee
And said, "Let be."

For to thee too the high Fates gave
Grace to be sacrificed and save,
That being arisen, in the equal sun,
God and the People should be one;
By those red roads thy footprints trod,
Man more divine, more human God,
Saviour; that where no light was known

But darkness, and a daytime flown,
Light should be shown.

Let there be light, O Italy!
For our feet falter in the night.
O lamp of living years to be,
O light of God, let there be light!
Fill with a love keener than flame
Men sealed in spirit with thy name,
The cities and the Roman skies,
Where men with other than man's eyes
Saw thy sun rise.

For theirs thou wast and thine were they
Whose names outshine thy very day;
For they are thine and theirs thou art
Whose blood beats living in man's heart,
Remembering ages fled and dead
Wherein for thy sake these men bled;
They that saw Trebia, they that see
Mentana, they in years to be
That shall see thee.

For thine are all of us, and ours
Thou; till the seasons bring to birth
A perfect people, and all the powers
Be with them that bear fruit on earth;
Till the inner heart of man be one
With freedom, and the sovereign sun;
And Time, in likeness of a guide,
Lead the Republic as a bride
Up to God's side.

COR CORDIUM

O heart of hearts, the chalice of love's fire,
Hid round with flowers and all the bounty of bloom;
O wonderful and perfect heart, for whom
The lyrist liberty made life a lyre;
O heavenly heart, at whose most dear desire
Dead love, living and singing, cleft his tomb,
And with him risen and regent in death's room
All day thy choral pulses rang full choir;
O heart whose beating blood was running song,
O sole thing sweeter than thine own songs were,
Help us for thy free love's sake to be free,

True for thy truth's sake, for thy strength's sake strong,
Till very liberty make clean and fair
The nursing earth as the sepulchral sea.

IN SAN LORENZO

Is thine hour come to wake, O slumbering Night?
Hath not the Dawn a message in thine ear?
Though thou be stone and sleep, yet shalt thou hear
When the word falls from heaven—Let there be light.
Thou knowest we would not do thee the despite
To wake thee while the old sorrow and shame were near;
We spake not loud for thy sake, and for fear
Lest thou shouldst lose the rest that was thy right,
The blessing given thee that was thine alone,
The happiness to sleep and to be stone:
Nay, we kept silence of thee for thy sake
Albeit we knew thee alive, and left with thee
The great good gift to feel not nor to see;
But will not yet thine Angel bid thee wake?

TIRESIAS

PART I

It is an hour before the hour of dawn.
Set in mine hand my staff and leave me here
Outside the hollow house that blind men fear,
More blind than I who live on life withdrawn
And feel on eyes that see not but foresee
The shadow of death which clothes Antigone.

Here lay her living body that here lies
Dead, if man living know what thing is death,
If life be all made up of blood and breath,
And no sense be save as of ears and eyes.
But heart there is not, tongue there is not found,
To think or sing what verge hath life or bound.

In the beginning when the powers that made
The young child man a little loved him, seeing
His joy of life and fair face of his being,
And bland and laughing with the man-child played,
As friends they saw on our divine one day

King Cadmus take to queen Harmonia.

The strength of soul that builds up as with hands
Walls spiritual and towers and towns of thought
Which only fate, not force, can bring to nought,
Took then to wife the light of all men's lands,
War's child and love's, most sweet and wise and strong,
Order of things and rule and guiding song.

It was long since: yea, even the sun that saw
Remembers hardly what was, nor how long.
And now the wise heart of the worldly song
Is perished, and the holy hand of law
Can set no tune on time, nor help again
The power of thought to build up life for men.

Yea, surely are they now transformed or dead,
And sleep below this world, where no sun warms,
Or move about it now in formless forms
Incognizable, and all their lordship fled;
And where they stood up singing crawl and hiss,
With fangs that kill behind their lips that kiss.

Yet though her marriage-garment, seeming fair,
Was dyed in sin and woven of jealousy
To turn their seed to poison, time shall see
The gods reissue from them, and repair
Their broken stamp of godhead, and again
Thought and wise love sing words of law to men.

I, Tiresias the prophet, seeing in Thebes
Much evil, and the misery of men's hands
Who sow with fruitless wheat the stones and sands,
With fruitful thorns the fallows and warm glebes,
Bade their hands hold lest worse hap came to pass;
But which of you had heed of Tiresias?

I am as Time's self in mine own wearied mind,
Whom the strong heavy-footed years have led
From night to night and dead men unto dead,
And from the blind hope to the memory blind;
For each man's life is woven, as Time's life is,
Of blind young hopes and old blind memories.

I am a soul outside of death and birth.
I see before me and afterward I see,
O child, O corpse, the live dead face of thee,
Whose life and death are one thing upon earth

Where day kills night and night again kills day
And dies; but where is that Harmonia?

O all-beholden light not seen of me,
Air, and warm winds that under the sun's eye
Stretch your strong wings at morning; and thou, sky,
Whose hollow circle engirdling earth and sea
All night the set stars limit, and all day
The moving sun remeasures; ye, I say,

Ye heights of hills, and thou Dircean spring
Inviolable, and ye towers that saw cast down
Seven kings keen-sighted toward your seven-faced town
And quenched the red seed of one sightless king;
And thou, for death less dreadful than for birth,
Whose wild leaves hide the horror of the earth,

O mountain whereon gods made chase of kings,
Cithæron, thou that sawest on Pentheus dead
Fangs of a mother fasten and wax red
And satiate with a son thy swollen springs,
And heardst her cry fright all thine eyries' nests
Who gave death suck at sanguine-suckling breasts;

Yea, and a grief more grievous, without name,
A curse too grievous for the name of grief,
Thou sawest, and heardst the rumour scare belief
Even unto death and madness, when the flame
Was lit whose ashes dropped about the pyre
That of two brethren made one sundering fire;

O bitter nurse, that on thine hard bare knees
Rear'dst for his fate the bloody-footed child
Whose hands should be more bloodily defiled
And the old blind feet walk wearier ways than these,
Whose seed, brought forth in darkness unto doom,
Should break as fire out of his mother's womb;

I bear you witness as ye bear to me,
Time, day, night, sun, stars, life, death, air, sea, earth,
And ye that round the human house of birth
Watch with veiled heads and weaponed hands, and see
Good things and evil, strengthless yet and dumb,
Sit in the clouds with cloudlike hours to come;

Ye forces without form and viewless powers
That have the keys of all our years in hold,
That prophesy too late with tongues of gold,

In a strange speech whose words are perished hours,
I witness to you what good things ye give
As ye to me what evil while I live.

What should I do to blame you, what to praise,
For floral hours and hours funereal?
What should I do to curse or bless at all
For winter-woven or summer-coloured days?
Curse he that will and bless you whoso can,
I have no common part in you with man.

I hear a springing water, whose quick sound
Makes softer the soft sunless patient air,
And the wind's hand is laid on my thin hair
Light as a lover's, and the grasses round
Have odours in them of green bloom and rain
Sweet as the kiss wherewith sleep kisses pain.

I hear the low sound of the spring of time
Still beating as the low live throb of blood,
And where its waters gather head and flood
I hear change moving on them, and the chime
Across them of reverberate wings of hours
Sounding, and feel the future air of flowers.

The wind of change is soft as snow, and sweet
The sense thereof as roses in the sun,
The faint wind springing with the springs that run,
The dim sweet smell of flowering hopes, and heat
Of unbeholden sunrise; yet how long
I know not, till the morning put forth song.

I prophesy of life, who live with death;
Of joy, being sad; of sunlight, who am blind;
Of man, whose ways are alien from mankind
And his lips are not parted with man's breath;
I am a word out of the speechless years,
The tongue of time, that no man sleeps who hears.

I stand a shadow across the door of doom,
Athwart the lintel of death's house, and wait;
Nor quick nor dead, nor flexible by fate,
Nor quite of earth nor wholly of the tomb;
A voice, a vision, light as fire or air,
Driven between days that shall be and that were.

I prophesy, with feet upon a grave,
Of death cast out and life devouring death

As flame doth wood and stubble with a breath;
Of freedom, though all manhood were one slave;
Of truth, though all the world were liar; of love,
That time nor hate can raze the witness of.

Life that was given for love's sake and his law's
Their powers have no more power on; they divide
Spoils wrung from lust or wrath of man or pride,
And keen oblivion without pity or pause
Sets them on fire and scatters them on air
Like ashes shaken from a suppliant's hair.

But life they lay no hand on; life once given
No force of theirs hath competence to take;
Life that was given for some divine thing's sake,
To mix the bitterness of earth with heaven,
Light with man's night, and music with his breath,
Dies not, but makes its living food of death.

I have seen this, who live where men are not,
In the high starless air of fruitful night
On that serenest and obscurest height
Where dead and unborn things are one in thought
And whence the live unconquerable springs
Feed full of force the torrents of new things.

I have seen this, who saw long since, being man,
As now I know not if indeed I be,
The fair bare body of Wisdom, good to see
And evil, whence my light and night began;
Light on the goal and darkness on the way,
Light all through night and darkness all through day.

Mother, that by that Pegasean spring 1
Didst fold round in thine arms thy blinded son,
Weeping "O holiest, what thing hast thou done,
What, to my child? woe's me that see the thing!
Is this thy love to me-ward, and hereof
Must I take sample how the gods can love?

"O child, thou hast seen indeed, poor child of mine,
The breasts and flanks of Pallas bare in sight,
But never shalt see more the dear sun's light;
O Helicon, how great a pay is thine
For some poor antelopes and wild-deer dead,
My child's eyes hast thou taken in their stead—"

Mother, thou knewest not what she had to give,

Thy goddess, though then angered, for mine eyes;
Fame and foreknowledge, and to be most wise,
And centuries of high-thoughted life to live,
And in mine hand this guiding staff to be
As eyesight to the feet of men that see.

Perchance I shall not die at all, nor pass
The general door and lintel of men dead;
Yet even the very tongue of wisdom said
What grace should come with death to Tiresias,
What special honour that God's hand accord
Who gathers all men's nations as their lord.

And sometimes when the secret eye of thought
Is changed with obscuration, and the sense
Aches with long pain of hollow prescience,
And fiery foresight with foresuffering bought
Seems even to infect my spirit and consume,
Hunger and thirst come on me for the tomb.

I could be fain to drink my death and sleep,
And no more wrapped about with bitter dreams
Talk with the stars and with the winds and streams
And with the inevitable years, and weep;
For how should he who communes with the years
Be sometime not a living spring of tears?

O child, that guided of thine only will
Didst set thy maiden foot against the gate
To strike it open ere thine hour of fate,
Antigone, men say not thou didst ill,
For love's sake and the reverence of his awe
Divinely dying, slain by mortal law;

For love is awful as immortal death.
And through thee surely hath thy brother won
Rest, out of sight of our world-weary sun,
And in the dead land where ye ghosts draw breath
A royal place and honour; so wast thou
Happy, though earth have hold of thee too now.

So hast thou life and name inviolable
And joy it may be, sacred and severe,
Joy secret-souled beyond all hope or fear,
A monumental joy wherein to dwell
Secluse and silent, a selected state,
Serene possession of thy proper fate.

Thou art not dead as these are dead who live
Full of blind years, a sorrow-shaken kind,
Nor as these are am I the prophet blind;
They have not life that have not heart to give
Life, nor have eyesight who lack heart to see
When to be not is better than to be.

O ye whom time but bears with for a span,
How long will ye be blind and dead, how long
Make your own souls part of your own soul's wrong?
Son of the word of the most high gods, man,
Why wilt thou make thine hour of light and breath
Emptier of all but shame than very death?

Fool, wilt thou live for ever? though thou care
With all thine heart for life to keep it fast,
Shall not thine hand forego it at the last?
Lo, thy sure hour shall take thee by the hair
Sleeping, or when thou knowest not, or wouldst fly;
And as men died much mightier shalt thou die.

Yea, they are dead, men much more worth than thou;
The savour of heroic lives that were,
Is it not mixed into thy common air?
The sense of them is shed about thee now:
Feel not thy brows a wind blowing from far?
Aches not thy forehead with a future star?

The light that thou may'st make out of thy name
Is in the wind of this same hour that drives,
Blown within reach but once of all men's lives;
And he that puts forth hand upon the flame
Shall have it for a garland on his head
To sign him for a king among the dead.

But these men that the lessening years behold,
Who sit the most part without flame or crown,
And brawl and sleep and wear their life-days down
With joys and griefs ignobler than of old,
And care not if the better day shall be—
Are these or art thou dead, Antigone?

PART II

As when one wakes out of a waning dream
And sees with instant eyes the naked thought
Whereof the vision as a web was wrought,

I saw beneath a heaven of cloud and gleam,
Ere yet the heart of the young sun waxed brave,
One like a prophet standing by a grave.

In the hoar heaven was hardly beam or breath,
And all the coloured hills and fields were grey,
And the wind wandered seeking for the day,
And wailed as though he had found her done to death
And this grey hour had built to bury her
The hollow twilight for a sepulchre.

But in my soul I saw as in a glass
A pale and living body full of grace
There lying, and over it the prophet's face
Fixed; and the face was not of Tiresias,
For such a starry fire was in his eyes
As though their light it was that made the skies.

Such eyes should God's have been when very love
Looked forth of them and set the sun aflame,
And such his lips that called the light by name
And bade the morning forth at sound thereof;
His face was sad and masterful as fate,
And like a star's his look compassionate.

Like a star's gazed on of sad eyes so long
It seems to yearn with pity, and all its fire
As a man's heart to tremble with desire
And heave as though the light would bring forth song;
Yet from his face flashed lightning on the land,
And like the thunder-bearer's was his hand.

The steepness of strange stairs had tired his feet,
And his lips yet seemed sick of that salt bread
Wherewith the lips of banishment are fed;
But nothing was there in the world so sweet
As the most bitter love, like God's own grace,
Wherewith he gazed on that fair buried face.

Grief and glad pride and passion and sharp shame,
Wrath and remembrance, faith and hope and hate
And pitiless pity of days degenerate,
Were in his eyes as an incorporate flame
That burned about her, and the heart thereof
And central flower was very fire of love.

But all about her grave wherein she slept
Were noises of the wild wind-footed years

Whose footprints flying were full of blood and tears,
Shrieks as of Maenads on their hills that leapt
And yelled as beasts of ravin, and their meat
Was the rent flesh of their own sons to eat:

And fiery shadows passing with strange cries,
And Sphinx-like shapes about the ruined lands,
And the red reek of parricidal hands
And intermixture of incestuous eyes,
And light as of that self-divided flame
Which made an end of the Cadmean name.

And I beheld again, and lo the grave,
And the bright body laid therein as dead,
And the same shadow across another head
That bowed down silent on that sleeping slave
Who was the lady of empire from her birth
And light of all the kingdoms of the earth.

Within the compass of the watcher's hand
All strengths of other men and divers powers
Were held at ease and gathered up as flowers;
His heart was as the heart of his whole land,
And at his feet as natural servants lay
Twilight and dawn and night and labouring day.

He was most awful of the sons of God.
Even now men seeing seemed at his lips to see
The trumpet of the judgment that should be,
And in his right hand terror for a rod,
And in the breath that made the mountains bow
The horned fire of Moses on his brow.

The strong wind of the coming of the Lord
Had blown as flame upon him, and brought down
On his bare head from heaven fire for a crown,
And fire was girt upon him as a sword
To smite and lighten, and on what ways he trod
There fell from him the shadow of a God.

Pale, with the whole world's judgment in his eyes,
He stood and saw the grief and shame endure
That he, though highest of angels might not cure,
And the same sins done under the same skies,
And the same slaves to the same tyrants thrown,
And fain he would have slept, and fain been stone.

But with unslumbering eyes he watched the sleep

That sealed her sense whose eyes were suns of old;
And the night shut and opened, and behold,
The same grave where those prophets came to weep,
But she that lay therein had moved and stirred,
And where those twain had watched her stood a third.

The tripled rhyme that closed in Paradise
With Love's name sealing up its starry speech—
The tripled might of hand that found in reach
All crowns beheld far off of all men's eyes,
Song, colour, carven wonders of live stone—
These were not, but the very soul alone.

The living spirit, the good gift of grace,
The faith which takes of its own blood to give
That the dead veins of buried hope may live,
Came on her sleeping, face to naked face,
And from a soul more sweet than all the south
Breathed love upon her sealed and breathless mouth.

Between her lips the breath was blown as fire,
And through her flushed veins leapt the liquid life,
And with sore passion and ambiguous strife
The new birth rent her and the new desire,
The will to live, the competence to be,
The sense to hearken and the soul to see.

And the third prophet standing by her grave
Stretched forth his hand and touched her, and her eyes
Opened as sudden suns in heaven might rise,
And her soul caught from his the faith to save;
Faith above creeds, faith beyond records, born
Of the pure, naked, fruitful, awful morn.

For in the daybreak now that night was dead
The light, the shadow, the delight, the pain,
The purpose and the passion of those twain,
Seemed gathered on that third prophetic head,
And all their crowns were as one crown, and one
His face with her face in the living sun.

For even with that communion of their eyes
His whole soul passed into her and made her strong;
And all the sounds and shows of shame and wrong,
The hand that slays, the lip that mocks and lies,
Temples and thrones that yet men seem to see—
Are these dead or art thou dead, Italy?

THE SONG OF THE STANDARD

Maiden most beautiful, mother most bountiful, lady of lands,
Queen and republican, crowned of the centuries whose years are thy sands,
See for thy sake what we bring to thee, Italy, here in our hands.

This is the banner thy gonfalon, fair in the front of thy fight,
Red from the hearts that were pierced for thee, white as thy mountains are white,
Green as the spring of thy soul everlasting, whose life-blood is light.

Take to thy bosom thy banner, a fair bird fit for the nest,
Feathered for flight into sunrise or sunset, for eastward or west,
Fledged for the flight everlasting, but held yet warm to thy breast.

Gather it close to thee, song-bird or storm-bearer, eagle or dove,
Lift it to sunward, a beacon beneath to the beacon above,
Green as our hope in it, white as our faith in it, red as our love.

Thunder and splendour of lightning are hid in the folds of it furled;
Who shall unroll it but thou, as thy bolt to be handled and hurled,
Out of whose lips is the honey, whose bosom the milk of the world?

Out of thine hands hast thou fed us with pasture of colour and song;
Glory and beauty by birthright to thee as thy garments belong;
Out of thine hands thou shalt give us as surely deliverance from wrong.

Out of thine eyes thou hast shed on us love as a lamp in our night,
Wisdom a lodestar to ships, and remembrance a flame-coloured light;
Out of thine eyes thou shalt shew us as surely the sun-dawn of right.

Turn to us, speak to us, Italy, mother, but once and a word,
None shall not follow thee, none shall not serve thee, not one that has heard;
Twice hast thou spoken a message, and time is athirst for the third.

Kingdom and empire of peoples thou hadst, and thy lordship made one
North sea and south sea and east men and west men that look on the sun;
Spirit was in thee and counsel, when soul in the nations was none.

Banner and beacon thou wast to the centuries of storm-wind and foam,
Ages that clashed in the dark with each other, and years without home;
Empress and prophetess wast thou, and what wilt thou now be, O Rome?

Ah, by the faith and the hope and the love that have need of thee now,
Shines not thy face with the forethought of freedom, and burns not thy brow?
Who is against her but all men? and who is beside her but thou?

Art thou not better than all men? and where shall she turn but to thee?
Lo, not a breath, not a beam, not a beacon from midland to sea;
Freedom cries out for a sign among nations, and none will be free.

England in doubt of her, France in despair of her, all without heart—
Stand on her side in the vanward of ages, and strike on her part!
Strike but one stroke for the love of her love of thee, sweet that thou art!

Take in thy right hand thy banner, a strong staff fit for thine hand;
Forth at the light of it lifted shall foul things flock from the land;
Faster than stars from the sun shall they fly, being lighter than sand.

Green thing to green in the summer makes answer, and rose-tree to rose;
Lily by lily the year becomes perfect; and none of us knows
What thing is fairest of all things on earth as it brightens and blows.

This thing is fairest in all time of all things, in all time is best—
Freedom, that made thee, our mother, and suckled her sons at thy breast;
Take to thy bosom the nations, and there shall the world come to rest.

ON THE DOWNS

A faint sea without wind or sun;
A sky like flameless vapour dun;
A valley like an unsealed grave
That no man cares to weep upon,
Bare, without boon to crave,
Or flower to save.
And on the lip's edge of the down,
Here where the bent-grass burns to brown
In the dry sea-wind, and the heath
Crawls to the cliff-side and looks down,
I watch, and hear beneath
The low tide breathe.

Along the long lines of the cliff,
Down the flat sea-line without skiff
Or sail or back-blown fume for mark,
Through wind-worn heads of heath and stiff
Stems blossomless and stark
With dry sprays dark,

I send mine eyes out as for news
Of comfort that all these refuse,
Tidings of light or living air
From windward where the low clouds muse

And the sea blind and bare
Seems full of care.

So is it now as it was then,
And as men have been such are men.
There as I stood I seem to stand,
Here sitting chambered, and again
Feel spread on either hand
Sky, sea, and land.

As a queen taken and stripped and bound
Sat earth, discoloured and discrowned;
As a king's palace empty and dead
The sky was, without light or sound;
And on the summer's head
Were ashes shed.

Scarce wind enough was on the sea,
Scarce hope enough there moved in me,
To sow with live blown flowers of white
The green plain's sad serenity,
Or with stray thoughts of light
Touch my soul's sight.

By footless ways and sterile went
My thought unsatisfied, and bent
With blank unspeculative eyes
On the untracked sands of discontent
Where, watched of helpless skies,
Life hopeless lies.

East and west went my soul to find
Light, and the world was bare and blind
And the soil herbless where she trod
And saw men laughing scourge mankind,
Unsmitten by the rod
Of any God.

Out of time's blind old eyes were shed
Tears that were mortal, and left dead
The heart and spirit of the years,
And on mans fallen and helmless head
Time's disanointing tears
Fell cold as fears.

Hope flowering had but strength to bear
The fruitless fruitage of despair;
Grief trod the grapes of joy for wine,

Whereof love drinking unaware
Died as one undivine
And made no sign.

And soul and body dwelt apart;
And weary wisdom without heart
Stared on the dead round heaven and sighed,
"Is death too hollow as thou art,
Or as man's living pride?"
And saying so died.

And my soul heard the songs and groans
That are about and under thrones,
And felt through all time's murmur thrill
Fate's old imperious semitones
That made of good and ill
One same tune still.

Then "Where is God? and where is aid?
Or what good end of these?" she said;
"Is there no God or end at all,
Nor reason with unreason weighed,
Nor force to disenthral
Weak feet that fall?

"No light to lighten and no rod
To chasten men? Is there no God?"
So girt with anguish, iron-zoned,
Went my soul weeping as she trod
Between the men enthroned
And men that groaned.

O fool, that for brute cries of wrong
Heard not the grey glad mother's song
Ring response from the hills and waves,
But heard harsh noises all day long
Of spirits that were slaves
And dwelt in graves.

The wise word of the secret earth
Who knows what life and death are worth,
And how no help and no control
Can speed or stay things come to birth,
Nor all worlds' wheels that roll
Crush one born soul.

With all her tongues of life and death,
With all her bloom and blood and breath,

From all years dead and all things done,
In the ear of man the mother saith,
"There is no God, O son,
If thou be none."

So my soul sick with watching heard
That day the wonder of that word,
And as one springs out of a dream
Sprang, and the stagnant wells were stirred
Whence flows through gloom and gleam
Thought's soundless stream.

Out of pale cliff and sunburnt health,
Out of the low sea curled beneath
In the land's bending arm embayed,
Out of all lives that thought hears breathe
Life within life inlaid,
Was answer made.

A multitudinous monotone
Of dust and flower and seed and stone,
In the deep sea-rock's mid-sea sloth,
In the live water's trembling zone,
In all men love and loathe,
One God at growth.

One forceful nature uncreate
That feeds itself with death and fate,
Evil and good, and change and time,
That within all men lies at wait
Till the hour shall bid them climb
And live sublime.

For all things come by fate to flower
At their unconquerable hour,
And time brings truth, and truth makes free,
And freedom fills time's veins with power,
As, brooding on that sea,
My thought filled me.

And the sun smote the clouds and slew,
And from the sun the sea's breath blew,
And white waves laughed and turned and fled
The long green heaving sea-field through,
And on them overhead
The sky burnt red

Like a furled flag that wind sets free,

On the swift summer-coloured sea
Shook out the red lines of the light,
The live sun's standard, blown to lee
Across the live sea's white
And green delight.

And with divine triumphant awe
My spirit moved within me saw,
With burning passion of stretched eyes,
Clear as the light's own firstborn law,
In windless wastes of skies
Time's deep dawn rise.

MESSIDOR

Put in the sickles and reap;
For the morning of harvest is red,
And the long large ranks of the corn
Coloured and clothed as the morn
Stand thick in the fields and deep
For them that faint to be fed.
Let all that hunger and weep
Come hither, and who would have bread
Put in the sickles and reap.
Coloured and clothed as the morn,
The grain grows ruddier than gold,
And the good strong sun is alight
In the mists of the day-dawn white,
And the crescent, a faint sharp horn,
In the fear of his face turns cold
As the snakes of the night-time that creep
From the flag of our faith unrolled.
Put in the sickles and reap.

In the mists of the day-dawn white
That roll round the morning star,
The large flame lightens and grows
Till the red-gold harvest-rows,
Full-grown, are full of the light
As the spirits of strong men are,
Crying, Who shall slumber or sleep?
Who put back morning or mar?
Put in the sickles and reap.

Till the red-gold harvest-rows
For miles through shudder and shine

In the wind's breath, fed with the sun,
A thousand spear-heads as one
Bowed as for battle to close
Line in rank against line
With place and station to keep
Till all men's hands at a sign
Put in the sickles and reap.

A thousand spear-heads as one
Wave as with swing of the sea
When the mid tide sways at its height;
For the hour is for harvest or fight
In face of the just calm sun,
As the signal in season may be
And the lot in the helm may leap
When chance shall shake it; but ye,
Put in the sickles and reap.

For the hour is for harvest or fight
To clothe with raiment of red;
O men sore stricken of hours,
Lo, this one, is not it ours
To glean, to gather, to smite?
Let none make risk of his head
Within reach of the clean scythe-sweep,
When the people that lay as the dead
Put in the sickles and reap.

Lo, this one, is not it ours,
Now the ruins of dead things rattle
As dead men's bones in the pit,
Now the kings wax lean as they sit
Girt round with memories of powers,
With musters counted as cattle
And armies folded as sheep
Till the red blind husbandman battle
Put in the sickles and reap?

Now the kings wax lean as they sit,
The people grow strong to stand;
The men they trod on and spat,
The dumb dread people that sat
As corpses cast in a pit,
Rise up with God at their hand,
And thrones are hurled on a heap,
And strong men, sons of the land,
Put in the sickles and reap.

The dumb dread people that sat
All night without screen for the night,
All day without food for the day,
They shall give not their harvest away,
They shall eat of its fruit and wax fat:
They shall see the desire of their sight,
Though the ways of the seasons be steep,
They shall climb with face to the light,
Put in the sickles and reap.

ODE ON THE INSURRECTION IN CANDIA

STROPHE I

I laid my laurel-leaf
At the white feet of grief,
Seeing how with covered face and plumeless wings,
With unreverted head
Veiled, as who mourns his dead,
Lay Freedom couched between the thrones of kings,
A wearied lion without lair,
And bleeding from base wounds, and vexed with alien air.

STROPHE II

Who was it, who, put poison to thy mouth,
Who lulled with craft or chant thy vigilant eyes,
O light of all men, lamp to north and south,
Eastward and westward, under all men's skies?
For if thou sleep, we perish, and thy name
Dies with the dying of our ephemeral breath;
And if the dust of death o'ergrows thy flame,
Heaven also is darkened with the dust of death.
If thou be mortal, if thou change or cease,
If thine hand fail, or thine eyes turn from Greece,
Thy firstborn, and the firstfruits of thy fame,
God is no God, and man is moulded out of shame.

STROPHE III

Is there change in the secret skies,
In the sacred places that see
The divine beginning of things,
The weft of the web of the world?

Is Freedom a worm that dies,
And God no God of the free?
Is heaven like as earth with her kings
And time as a serpent curled
Round life as a tree?

From the steel-bound snows of the north,
From the mystic mother, the east,
From the sands of the fiery south,
From the low-lit clouds of the west,
A sound of a cry is gone forth;
Arise, stand up from the feast,
Let wine be far from the mouth,
Let no man sleep or take rest,
Till the plague hath ceased.

Let none rejoice or make mirth
Till the evil thing be stayed,
Nor grief be lulled in the lute,
Nor hope be loud on the lyre;
Let none be glad upon earth.
O music of young man and maid,
O songs of the bride, be mute.
For the light of her eyes, her desire,
Is the soul dismayed.

It is not a land new-born
That is scourged of a stranger's hand,
That is rent and consumed with flame.
We have known it of old, this face,
With the cheeks and the tresses torn,
With shame on the brow as a brand.
We have named it of old by name,
The land of the royallest race,
The most holy land.

STROPHE IV

Had I words of fire,
Whose words are weak as snow;
Were my heart a lyre
Whence all its love might flow
In the mighty modulations of desire,
In the notes wherewith man's passion worships woe;

Could my song release
The thought weak words confine,

And my grief, O Greece,
Prove how it worships thine;
It would move with pulse of war the limbs of peace,
Till she flushed and trembled and became divine.

(Once she held for true
This truth of sacred strain;
Though blood drip like dew
And life run down like rain,
It is better that war spare but one or two
Than that many live, and liberty be slain.)

Then with fierce increase
And bitter mother's mirth,
From the womb of peace,
A womb that yearns for birth,
As a man-child should deliverance come to Greece,
As a saviour should the child be born on earth.

STROPHE V

O that these my days had been
Ere white peace and shame were wed
Without torch or dancers' din
Round the unsacred marriage-bed!
For of old the sweet-tongued law,
Freedom, clothed with all men's love,
Girt about with all men's awe,
With the wild war-eagle mated
The white breast of peace the dove,
And his ravenous heart abated
And his windy wings were furled
In an eyrie consecrated
Where the snakes of strife uncurled,
And her soul was soothed and sated
With the welfare of the world.

ANTISTROPHE I

But now, close-clad with peace,
While war lays hand on Greece,
The kingdoms and their kings stand by to see;
"Aha, we are strong," they say,
"We are sure, we are well," even they;
"And if we serve, what ails ye to be free?
We are warm, clothed round with peace and shame;

But ye lie dead and naked, dying for a name."

ANTISTROPHE II

O kings and queens and nations miserable,
O fools and blind, and full of sins and fears,
With these it is, with you it is not well;
Ye have one hour, but these the immortal years.
These for a pang, a breath, a pulse of pain,
Have honour, while that honour on earth shall be:
Ye for a little sleep and sloth shall gain
Scorn, while one man of all men born is free.
Even as the depth more deep than night or day,
The sovereign heaven that keeps its eldest way,
So without chance or change, so without stain,
The heaven of their high memories shall nor wax nor wane.

ANTISTROPHE III

As the soul on the lips of the dead
Stands poising her wings for flight,
A bird scarce quit of her prison,
But fair without form or flesh,
So stands over each man's head
A splendour of imminent light,
A glory of fame rearisen,
Of day rearisen afresh
From the hells of night.

In the hundred cities of Crete
Such glory was not of old,
Though her name was great upon earth
And her face was fair on the sea.
The words of her lips were sweet,
Her days were woven with gold,
Her fruits came timely to birth;
So fair she was, being free,
Who is bought and sold.

So fair, who is fairer now
With her children dead at her side,
Unsceptred, unconsecrated,
Unapparelled, unhelped, unpitied,
With blood for gold on her brow,
Where the towery tresses divide;
The goodly, the golden-gated,

Many-crowned, many-named, many-citied,
Made like as a bride.

And these are the bridegroom's gifts;
Anguish that straitens the breath,
Shame, and the weeping of mothers,
And the suckling dead at the breast,
White breast that a long sob lifts;
And the dumb dead mouth, which saith,
"How long, and how long, my brothers?"
And wrath which endures not rest,
And the pains of death.

ANTISTROPHE IV

Ah, but would that men,
With eyelids purged by tears,
Saw, and heard again
With consecrated ears,
All the clamour, all the splendour, all the slain,
All the lights and sounds of war, the fates and fears;

Saw far off aspire,
With crash of mine and gate,
From a single pyre
The myriad flames of fate,
Soul by soul transfigured in funereal fire,
Hate made weak by love, and love made strong by hate.

Children without speech,
And many a nursing breast;
Old men in the breach,
Where death sat down a guest;
With triumphant lamentation made for each,
Let the world salute their ruin and their rest.

In one iron hour
The crescent flared and waned,
As from tower to tower,
Fire-scathed and sanguine-stained,
Death, with flame in hand, an open bloodred flower,
Passed, and where it bloomed no bloom of life remained.

ANTISTROPHE V

Hear, thou earth, the heavy-hearted

Weary nurse of waning races;
From the dust of years departed,
From obscure funereal places,
Raise again thy sacred head,
Lift the light up of thine eyes
Where are they of all thy dead
That did more than these men dying
In their godlike Grecian wise?
Not with garments rent and sighing,
Neither gifts of myrrh and gold,
Shall their sons lament them lying,
Lest the fame of them wax cold;
But with lives to lives replying,
And a worship from of old.

EPODE

O sombre heart of earth and swoln with grief,
That in thy time wast as a bird for mirth,
Dim womb of life and many a seed and sheaf,
And full of changes, ancient heart of earth,
From grain and flower, from grass and every leaf,
Thy mysteries and thy multitudes of birth,
From hollow and hill, from vales and all thy springs,
From all shapes born and breath of all lips made,
From thunders, and the sound of winds and wings,
From light, and from the solemn sleep of shade,
From the full fountains of all living things,
Speak, that this plague be stayed.
Bear witness all the ways of death and life
If thou be with us in the world's old strife,
If thou be mother indeed,
And from these wounds that bleed
Gather in thy great breast the dews that fall,
And on thy sacred knees
Lull with mute melodies,
Mother, thy sleeping sons in death's dim hall.
For these thy sons, behold,
Sons of thy sons of old,
Bear witness if these be not as they were;
If that high name of Greece
Depart, dissolve, decease
From mouths of men and memories like as air.
By the last milk that drips
Dead on the child's dead lips,
By old men's white unviolated hair,
By sweet unburied faces

That fill those red high places
Where death and freedom found one lion's lair,
By all the bloodred tears
That fill the chaliced years,
The vessels of the sacrament of time,
Wherewith, O thou most holy,
O Freedom, sure and slowly
Thy ministrant white hands cleanse earth of crime;
Though we stand off afar
Where slaves and slaveries are,
Among the chains and crowns of poisonous peace;
Though not the beams that shone
From rent Arcadion
Can melt her mists and bid her snows decrease;
Do thou with sudden wings
Darken the face of kings,
But turn again the beauty of thy brows on Greece;
Thy white and woundless brows,
Whereto her great heart bows;
Give her the glories of thine eyes to see;
Turn thee, O holiest head,
Toward all thy quick and dead,
For love's sake of the souls that cry for thee;
O love, O light, O flame,
By thine own Grecian name,
We call thee and we charge thee that all these be free.

Jan. 1867.

"NON DOLET"

It does not hurt. She looked along the knife
Smiling, and watched the thick drops mix and run
Down the sheer blade; not that which had been done
Could hurt the sweet sense of the Roman wife,
But that which was to do yet ere the strife
Could end for each for ever, and the sun:
Nor was the palm yet nor was peace yet won
While pain had power upon her husband's life.
It does not hurt, Italia. Thou art more
Than bride to bridegroom; how shalt thou not take
The gift love's blood has reddened for thy sake?
Was not thy lifeblood given for us before?
And if love's heartblood can avail thy need,
And thou not die, how should it hurt indeed?

EURYDICE

To Victor Hugo

Orpheus, the night is full of tears and cries,
And hardly for the storm and ruin shed
Can even thine eyes be certain of her head
Who never passed out of thy spirit's eyes,
But stood and shone before them in such wise
As when with love her lips and hands were fed,
And with mute mouth out of the dusty dead
Strove to make answer when thou bad'st her rise.
Yet viper-stricken must her lifeblood feel
The fang that stung her sleeping, the foul germ
Even when she wakes of hell's most poisonous worm,
Though now it writhe beneath her wounded heel.
Turn yet, she will not fade nor fly from thee;
Wait, and see hell yield up Eurydice.

AN APPEAL

I

Art thou indeed among these,
Thou of the tyrannous crew,
The kingdoms fed upon blood,
O queen from of old of the seas,
England, art thou of them too
That drink of the poisonous flood,
That hide under poisonous trees?

II

Nay, thy name from of old,
Mother, was pure, or we dreamed
Purer we held thee than this,
Purer fain would we hold;
So goodly a glory it seemed,
A fame so bounteous of bliss,
So more precious than gold.

III

A praise so sweet in our ears,
That thou in the tempest of things
As a rock for a refuge shouldst stand,
In the bloodred river of tears
Poured forth for the triumph of kings;
A safeguard, a sheltering land,
In the thunder and torrent of years.

IV

Strangers came gladly to thee,
Exiles, chosen of men,
Safe for thy sake in thy shade,
Sat down at thy feet and were free.
So men spake of thee then;
Now shall their speaking be stayed?
Ah, so let it not be!

V

Not for revenge or affright,
Pride, or a tyrannous lust,
Cast from thee the crown of thy praise.
Mercy was thine in thy might;
Strong when thou wert, thou wert just;
Now, in the wrong-doing days,
Cleave thou, thou at least, to the right.

VI

How should one charge thee, how sway,
Save by the memories that were?
Not thy gold nor the strength of thy ships,
Nor the might of thine armies at bay,
Made thee, mother, most fair;
But a word from republican lips
Said in thy name in thy day.

VII

Hast thou said it, and hast thou forgot?
Is thy praise in thine ears as a scoff?
Blood of men guiltless was shed,
Children, and souls without spot,

Shed, but in places far off;
Let slaughter no more be, said
Milton; and slaughter was not.

VIII

Was it not said of thee too,
Now, but now, by thy foes,
By the slaves that had slain their France,
And thee would slay as they slew—
"Down with her walls that enclose
Freemen that eye us askance,
Fugitives, men that are true!"

IX

This was thy praise or thy blame
From bondsman or freeman—to be
Pure from pollution of slaves,
Clean of their sins, and thy name
Bloodless, innocent, free;
Now if thou be not, thy waves
Wash not from off thee thy shame.

X

Freeman he is not, but slave,
Whoso in fear for the State
Cries for surety of blood,
Help of gibbet and grave;
Neither is any land great
Whom, in her fear-stricken mood,
These things only can save.

XI

Lo, how fair from afar,
Taintless of tyranny, stands
Thy mighty daughter, for years
Who trod the winepress of war;
Shines with immaculate hands;
Slays not a foe, neither fears;
Stains not peace with a scar.

Be not as tyrant or slave,
England; be not as these,
Thou that wert other than they.
Stretch out thine hand, but to save;
Put forth thy strength, and release;
Lest there arise, if thou slay,
Thy shame as a ghost from the grave.

November 20, 1867.

PERINDE AC CADAVER

In a vision Liberty stood
By the childless charm-stricken bed
Where, barren of glory and good,
Knowing nought if she would not or would,
England slept with her dead.
Her face that the foam had whitened,
Her hands that were strong to strive,
Her eyes whence battle had lightened,
Over all was a drawn shroud tightened
To bind her asleep and alive.

She turned and laughed in her dream
With grey lips arid and cold;
She saw not the face as a beam
Burn on her, but only a gleam
Through her sleep as of new-stamped gold.

But the goddess, with terrible tears
In the light of her down-drawn eyes,
Spake fire in the dull sealed ears;
"Thou, sick with slumbers and fears,
Wilt thou sleep now indeed or arise?

"With dreams and with words and with light
Memories and empty desires
Thou hast wrapped thyself round all night;
Thou hast shut up thine heart from the right,
And warmed thee at burnt-out fires.

"Yet once if I smote at thy gate,
Thy sons would sleep not, but heard;

O thou that wast found so great,
Art thou smitten with folly or fate
That thy sons have forgotten my word?

O Cromwell's mother, O breast
That suckled Milton! thy name
That was beautiful then, that was blest,
Is it wholly discrowned and deprest,
Trodden under by sloth into shame?

"Why wilt thou hate me and die?
For none can hate me and live.
What ill have I done to thee? why
Wilt thou turn from me fighting, and fly,
Who would follow thy feet and forgive?

"Thou hast seen me stricken, and said,
What is it to me? I am strong:
Thou hast seen me bowed down on my dead
And laughed and lifted thine head,
And washed thine hands of my wrong.

"Thou hast put out the soul of thy sight;
Thou hast sought to my foemen as friend,
To my traitors that kiss me and smite,
To the kingdoms and empires of night
That begin with the darkness, and end.

"Turn thee, awaken, arise,
With the light that is risen on the lands,
With the change of the fresh-coloured skies;
Set thine eyes on mine eyes,
Lay thy hands in my hands."

She moved and mourned as she heard,
Sighed and shifted her place,
As the wells of her slumber were stirred
By the music and wind of the word,
Then turned and covered her face.

"Ah," she said in her sleep,
"Is my work not done with and done?
Is there corn for my sickle to reap?
And strange is the pathway, and steep,
And sharp overhead is the sun.

"I have done thee service enough,
Loved thee enough in my day;

Now nor hatred nor love
Nor hardly remembrance thereof
Lives in me to lighten my way.

"And is it not well with us here?
Is change as good as is rest?
What hope should move me, or fear,
That eye should open or ear,
Who have long since won what is best?

"Where among us are such things
As turn men's hearts into hell?
Have we not queens without stings,
Scotched princes, and fangless kings?
Yea," she said, "we are well.

"We have filed the teeth of the snake
Monarchy, how should it bite?
Should the slippery slow thing wake,
It will not sting for my sake;
Yea," she said, "I do right."

So spake she, drunken with dreams,
Mad; but again in her ears
A voice as of storm-swelled streams
Spake; "No brave shame then redeems
Thy lusts of sloth and thy fears?

"Thy poor lie slain of thine hands,
Their starved limbs rot in thy sight;
As a shadow the ghost of thee stands
Among men living and lands,
And stirs not leftward or right.

"Freeman he is not, but slave,
Who stands not out on my side;
His own hand hollows his grave,
Nor strength is in me to save
Where strength is none to abide.

"Time shall tread on his name
That was written for honour of old,
Who hath taken in change for fame
Dust, and silver, and shame,
Ashes, and iron, and gold."

MONOTONES

Because there is but one truth;
Because there is but one banner;
Because there is but one light;
Because we have with us our youth
Once, and one chance and one manner
Of service, and then the night;
Because we have found not yet
Any way for the world to follow
Save only that ancient way;
Whosoever forsake or forget,
Whose faith soever be hollow,
Whose hope soever grow grey;

Because of the watchwords of kings
That are many and strange and unwritten,
Diverse, and our watchword is one;
Therefore, though seven be the strings,
One string, if the harp be smitten,
Sole sounds, till the tune be done;

Sounds without cadence or change
In a weary monotonous burden,
Be the keynote of mourning or mirth;
Free, but free not to range;
Taking for crown and for guerdon
No man's praise upon earth;

Saying one sole word evermore,
In the ears of the charmed world saying,
Charmed by spells to its death;
One that chanted of yore
To a tune of the sword-sweep's playing
In the lips of the dead blew breath;

Therefore I set not mine hand
To the shifting of changed modulations,
To the smiting of manifold strings;
While the thrones of the throned men stand,
One song for the morning of nations,
One for the twilight of kings.

One chord, one word, and one way,
One hope as our law, one heaven,
Till slain be the great one wrong;
Till the people it could not slay,
Risen up, have for one star seven,

For a single, a sevenfold song.

THE OBLATION

ASK nothing more of me, sweet;
All I can give you I give.
Heart of my heart, were it more,
More would be laid at your feet:
Love that should help you to live,
Song that should spur you to soar.
All things were nothing to give
Once to have sense of you more,
Touch you and taste of you sweet,
Think you and breathe you and live,
Swept of your wings as they soar,
Trodden by chance of your feet.

I that have love and no more
Give you but love of you, sweet:
He that hath more, let him give;
He that hath wings, let him soar;
Mine is the heart at your feet
Here, that must love you to live.

A YEAR'S BURDEN

1870

Fire and wild light of hope and doubt and fear,
Wind of swift change, and clouds and hours that veer
As the storm shifts of the tempestuous year;
Cry wellaway, but well befall the right.
Hope sits yet hiding her war-wearied eyes,
Doubt sets her forehead earthward and denies,
But fear brought hand to hand with danger dies,
Dies and is burnt up in the fire of fight.

Hearts bruised with loss and eaten through with shame
Turn at the time's touch to devouring flame;
Grief stands as one that knows not her own name,
Nor if the star she sees bring day or night.

No song breaks with it on the violent air,
But shrieks of shame, defeat, and brute despair;

Yet something at the star's heart far up there
Burns as a beacon in our shipwrecked sight.

O strange fierce light of presage, unknown star,
Whose tongue shall tell us what thy secrets are,
What message trembles in thee from so far?
Cry wellaway. but well befall the right.

From shores laid waste across an iron sea
Where the waifs drift of hopes that were to be,
Across the red rolled foam we look for thee,
Across the fire we look up for the light.

From days laid waste across disastrous years,
From hopes cut down across a world of fears,
We gaze with eyes too passionate for tears,
Where faith abides though hope be put to flight.

Old hope is dead, the grey-haired hope grown blind
That talked with us of old things out of mind,
Dreams, deeds and men the world has left behind;
Yet, though hope die, faith lives in hope's despite.

Ay, with hearts fixed on death and hopeless hands
We stand about our banner while it stands
Above but one field of the ruined lands;
Cry wellaway, but well befall the right.

Though France were given for prey to bird and beast,
Though Rome were rent in twain of king and priest,
The soul of man, the soul is safe at least
That gives death life and dead men hands to smite.

Are ye so strong, O kings, O strong men? Nay,
Waste all ye will and gather all ye may,
Yet one thing is there that ye shall not slay,
Even thought, that fire nor iron can affright.

The woundless and invisible thought that goes
Free throughout time as north or south wind blows,
Far throughout space as east or west sea flows,
And all dark things before it are made bright.

Thy thought, thy word, O soul republican,
O spirit of life, O God whose name is man:
What sea of sorrows but thy sight shall span?
Cry wellaway, but well befall the right.

With all its coils crushed, all its rings uncurled,
The one most poisonous worm that soiled the world
Is wrenched from off the throat of man, and hurled
Into deep hell from empire's helpless height.

Time takes no more infection of it now;
Like a dead snake divided of the plough,
The rotten thing lies cut in twain; but thou,
Thy fires shall heal us of the serpent's bite.

Ay, with red cautery and a burning brand
Purge thou the leprous leaven of the land;
Take to thee fire, and iron in thine hand,
Till blood and tears have washed the soiled limbs white.

We have sinned against thee in dreams and wicked sleep;
Smite, we will shrink not; strike, we will not weep;
Let the heart feel thee; let thy wound go deep;
Cry wellaway, but well befall the right.

Wound us with love, pierce us with longing, make
Our souls thy sacrifices; turn and take
Our hearts for our sin-offerings lest they break,
And mould them with thine hands and give them might.

Then, when the cup of ills is drained indeed,
Will we come to thee with our wounds that bleed,
With famished mouths and hearts that thou shalt feed,
And see thee worshipped as the world's delight.

There shall be no more wars nor kingdoms won,
But in thy sight whose eyes are as the sun
All names shall be one name, all nations one,
All souls of men in man's one soul unite.

O sea whereon men labour, O great sea
That heaven seems one with, shall these things not be?
O earth, our earth, shall time not make us free?
Cry wellaway, but well befall the right.

EPILOGUE

Between the wave-ridge and the strand
I let you forth in sight of land,
Songs that with storm-crossed wings and eyes
Strain eastward till the darkness dies;

Let signs and beacons fall or stand,
And stars and balefires set and rise;
Ye, till some lordlier lyric hand
Weave the beloved brows their crown,
At the beloved feet lie down.
O, whatsoever of life or light
Love hath to give you, what of might
Or heart or hope is yours to live,
I charge you take in trust to give
For very love's sake, in whose sight,
Through poise of hours alternative
And seasons plumed with light or night,
Ye live and move and have your breath
To sing with on the ridge of death.

I charge you faint not all night through
For love's sake that was breathed on you
To be to you as wings and feet
For travel, and as blood to heat
And sense of spirit to renew
And bloom of fragrance to keep sweet
And fire of purpose to keep true
The life, if life in such things be,
That I would give you forth of me.

Out where the breath of war may bear,
Out in the rank moist reddened air
That sounds and smells of death, and hath
No light but death's upon its path
Seen through the black wind's tangled hair,
I send you past the wild time's wrath
To find his face who bade you bear
Fruit of his seed to faith and love,
That he may take the heart thereof.

By day or night, by sea or street,
Fly till ye find and clasp his feet
And kiss as worshippers who bring
Too much love on their lips to sing,
But with hushed heads accept and greet
The presence of some heavenlier thing
In the near air; so may ye meet
His eyes, and droop not utterly
For shame's sake at the light you see.

Not utterly struck spiritless
For shame's sake and unworthiness
Of these poor forceless hands that come

Empty, these lips that should be dumb,
This love whose seal can but impress
These weak word-offerings wearisome
Whose blessings have not strength to bless
Nor lightnings fire to burn up aught
Nor smite with thunders of their thought.

One thought they have, even love; one light,
Truth, that keeps clear the sun by night;
One chord, of faith as of a lyre;
One heat, of hope as of a fire;
One heart, one music, and one might,
One flame, one altar, and one choir;
And one man's living head in sight
Who said, when all time's sea was foam,
"Let there be Rome"—and there was Rome.

As a star set in space for token
Like a live word of God's mouth spoken,
Visible sound, light audible,
In the great darkness thick as hell
A stanchless flame of love unsloken,
A sign to conquer and compel,
A law to stand in heaven unbroken
Whereby the sun shines, and wherethrough
Time's eldest empires are made new;

So rose up on our generations
That light of the most ancient nations,
Law, life, and light, on the world's way,
The very God of very day,
The sun-god; from their star-like stations
Far down the night in disarray
Fled, crowned with fires of tribulations,
The suns of sunless years, whose light
And life and law were of the night.

The naked kingdoms quenched and stark
Drave with their dead things down the dark,
Helmless; their whole world, throne by throne,
Fell, and its whole heart turned to stone,
Hopeless; their hands that touched our ark
Withered; and lo, aloft, alone,
On time's white waters man's one bark,
Where the red sundawn's open eye
Lit the soft gulf of low green sky.

So for a season piloted

It sailed the sunlight, and struck red
With fire of dawn reverberate
The wan face of incumbent fate
That paused half pitying overhead
And almost had foregone the freight
Of those dark hours the next day bred
For shame, and almost had forsworn
Service of night for love of morn.

Then broke the whole night in one blow,
Thundering; then all hell with one throe
Heaved, and brought forth beneath the stroke
Death; and all dead things moved and woke
That the dawn's arrows had brought low,
At the great sound of night that broke
Thundering, and all the old world-wide woe;
And under night's loud-sounding dome
Men sought her, and she was not Rome.

Still with blind hands and robes blood-wet
Night hangs on heaven, reluctant yet,
With black blood dripping from her eyes [1]
On the soiled lintels of the skies,
With brows and lips that thirst and threat,
Heart-sick with fear lest the sun rise,
And aching with her fires that set,
And shuddering ere dawn bursts her bars,
Burns out with all her beaten stars.

In this black wind of war they fly
Now, ere that hour be in the sky
That brings back hope, and memory back,
And light and law to lands that lack;
That spiritual sweet hour whereby
The bloody-handed night and black
Shall be cast out of heaven to die;
Kingdom by kingdom, crown by crown,
The fires of darkness are blown down.

Yet heavy, grievous yet the weight
Sits on us of imperfect fate.
From wounds of other days and deeds
Still this day's breathing body bleeds;
Still kings for fear and slaves for hate
Sow lives of men on earth like seeds
In the red soil they saturate;
And we, with faces eastward set,
Stand sightless of the morning yet.

And many for pure sorrow's sake
Look back and stretch back hands to take
Gifts of night's giving, ease and sleep,
Flowers of night's grafting, strong to steep
The soul in dreams it will not break,
Songs of soft hours that sigh and sweep
Its lifted eyelids nigh to wake
With subtle plumes and lulling breath
That soothe its weariness to death.

And many, called of hope and pride,
Fall ere the sunrise from our side.
Fresh lights and rumours of fresh fames
That shift and veer by night like flames,
Shouts and blown trumpets, ghosts that glide
Calling, and hail them by dead names,
Fears, angers, memories, dreams divide
Spirit from spirit, and wear out
Strong hearts of men with hope and doubt.

Till time beget and sorrow bear
The soul-sick eyeless child despair,
That comes among us, mad and blind,
With counsels of a broken mind,
Tales of times dead and woes that were,
And, prophesying against mankind,
Shakes out the horror of her hair
To take the sunlight with its coils
And hold the living soul in toils.

By many ways of death and moods
Souls pass into their servitudes.
Their young wings weaken, plume by plume
Drops, and their eyelids gather gloom
And close against man's frauds and feuds,
And their tongues call they know not whom
To help in their vicissitudes;
For many slaveries are, but one
Liberty, single as the sun.

One light, one law, that burns up strife,
And one sufficiency of life.
Self-stablished, the sufficing soul
Hears the loud wheels of changes roll,
Sees against man man bare the knife,
Sees the world severed, and is whole;
Sees force take dowerless fraud to wife,

And fear from fraud's incestuous bed
Crawl forth and smite his father dead:

Sees death made drunk with war, sees time
Weave many-coloured crime with crime,
State overthrown on ruining state,
And dares not be disconsolate.
Only the soul hath feet to climb,
Only the soul hath room to wait,
Hath brows and eyes to hold sublime
Above all evil and all good,
All strength and all decrepitude.

She only, she since earth began,
The many-minded soul of man,
From one incognizable root
That bears such divers-coloured fruit,
Hath ruled for blessing or for ban
The flight of seasons and pursuit;
She regent, she republican,
With wide and equal eyes and wings
Broods on things born and dying things.

Even now for love or doubt of us
The hour intense and hazardous
Hangs high with pinions vibrating
Whereto the light and darkness cling,
Dividing the dim season thus,
And shakes from one ambiguous wing
Shadow, and one is luminous,
And day falls from it; so the past
Torments the future to the last.

And we that cannot hear or see
The sounds and lights of liberty,
The witness of the naked God
That treads on burning hours unshod
With instant feet unwounded; we
That can trace only where he trod
By fire in heaven or storm at sea,
Not know the very present whole
And naked nature of the soul;

We that see wars and woes and kings,
And portents of enormous things,
Empires, and agonies, and slaves,
And whole flame of town-swallowing graves;
That hear the harsh hours clap sharp wings

Above the roar of ranks like waves,
From wreck to wreck as the world swings;
Know but that men there are who see
And hear things other far than we.

By the light sitting on their brows,
The fire wherewith their presence glows,
The music falling with their feet,
The sweet sense of a spirit sweet
That with their speech or motion grows
And breathes and burns men's hearts with heat;
By these signs there is none but knows
Men who have life and grace to give,
Men who have seen the soul and live.

By the strength sleeping in their eyes,
The lips whereon their sorrow lies
Smiling, the lines of tears unshed,
The large divine look of one dead
That speaks out of the breathless skies
In silence, when the light is shed
Upon man's soul of memories;
The supreme look that sets love free,
The look of stars and of the sea;

By the strong patient godhead seen
Implicit in their mortal mien,
The conscience of a God held still
And thunders ruled by their own will
And fast-bound fires that might burn clean
This worldly air that foul things fill,
And the afterglow of what has been,
That, passing, shows us without word
What they have seen, what they have heard,

By all these keen and burning signs
The spirit knows them and divines.
In bonds, in banishment, in grief,
Scoffed at and scourged with unbelief,
Foiled with false trusts and thwart designs,
Stripped of green days and hopes in leaf,
Their mere bare body of glory shines
Higher, and man gazing surelier sees
What light, what comfort is of these.

So I now gazing; till the sense
Being set on fire of confidence
Strains itself sunward, feels out far

Beyond the bright and morning star,
Beyond the extreme wave's refluence,
To where the fierce first sunbeams are
Whose fire intolerant and intense
As birthpangs whence day burns to be
Parts breathless heaven from breathing sea.

I see not, know not, and am blest,
Master, who know that thou knowest,
Dear lord and leader, at whose hand
The first days and the last days stand,
With scars and crowns on head and breast,
That fought for love of the sweet land
Or shall fight in her latter quest;
All the days armed and girt and crowned
Whose glories ring thy glory round.

Thou sawest, when all the world was blind,
The light that should be of mankind,
The very day that was to be;
And how shalt thou not sometime see
Thy city perfect to thy mind
Stand face to living face with thee,
And no miscrowned man's head behind;
The hearth of man, the human home,
The central flame that shall be Rome?

As one that ere a June day rise
Makes seaward for the dawn, and tries
The water with delighted limbs
That taste the sweet dark sea, and swims
Right eastward under strengthening skies,
And sees the gradual rippling rims
Of waves whence day breaks blossom-wise
Take fire ere light peer well above,
And laughs from all his heart with love;

And softlier swimming with raised head
Feels the full flower of morning shed
And fluent sunrise round him rolled
That laps and laves his body bold
With fluctuant heaven in water's stead,
And urgent through the growing gold
Strikes, and sees all the spray flash red,
And his soul takes the sun, and yearns
For joy wherewith the sea's heart burns;

So the soul seeking through the dark

Heavenward, a dove without an ark,
Transcends the unnavigable sea
Of years that wear out memory;
So calls, a sunward-singing lark,
In the ear of souls that should be free;
So points them toward the sun for mark
Who steer not for the stress of waves,
And seek strange helmsmen, and are slaves.

For if the swimmer's eastward eye
Must see no sunrise—must put by
The hope that lifted him and led
Once, to have light about his head,
To see beneath the clear low sky
The green foam-whitened wave wax red
And all the morning's banner fly—
Then, as earth's helpless hopes go down,
Let earth's self in the dark tides drown.

Yea, if no morning must behold
Man, other than were they now cold,
And other deeds than past deeds done,
Nor any near or far-off sun
Salute him risen and sunlike-souled,
Free, boundless, fearless, perfect, one,
Let man's world die like worlds of old,
And here in heaven's sight only be
The sole sun on the worldless sea.

[1.] AEsch. Cho. 1058.

Algernon Charles Swinburne – A Short Biography

Algernon Charles Swinburne was born at 7 Chester Street, Grosvenor Place, in London, on April 5th, 1837. He was the eldest of six children born to Captain Charles Henry Swinburne and Lady Jane Henrietta, daughter of the 3rd Earl of Ashburnham, a wealthy Northumbrian family.

Swinburne spent his early years at East Dene in Bonchurch, on the Isle of Wight. As a child, Swinburne was nervous and frail, but also imbued with a nervous energy and fearlessness almost to the point of recklessness.

He was schooled at Eton College from 1849 to 1853. It was here that he first began to write poetry. He excelled at languages and whilst still at Eton won first prizes in both French and Italian.

From Eton he moved to Oxford where he attended at Balliol College from 1856. Here he met friends to whom he became closely attached, among them Dante Gabriel Rossetti, William Morris and Edward

Burne-Jones, who in 1857, were painting their Arthurian murals on the walls of the Oxford Union. At Oxford Swinburne was mentored by Benjamin Jowett, the master of Balliol College, who recognised his poetic talent and, intervening on his behalf, tried to keep him from being expelled when he celebrated the Italian patriot Orsini, and his failed attempt on the life of Napoleon III in 1858. Swinburne had to leave the Universcity for a few months due to this but returned in May, 1860 but never received a degree.

Summers were usually spent at Capheaton Hall in Northumberland, the house of his grandfather, Sir John Swinburne, 6th Baronet, who had a famous library and was himself President of the Literary and Philosophical Society in Newcastle upon Tyne.

Swinburne proudly considered himself a native of Northumberland and this is reflected in poems such as the intensely patriotic 'Northumberland' and 'Grace Darling'. He enjoyed riding across the moors and was, it was said, a daring horseman, as he moved 'through honeyed leagues of the northland border', as he remembered the Scottish border in his Recollections.

In the period from 1857 to 1860, Swinburne was one of a number of Pre-Raphaelite's who visited and became part of Lady Pauline Trevelyan's intellectual circle at Wallington Hall, a few miles west of Morpeth in Northumberland.

After leaving college, he moved to London and began his career in earnest as well as becoming a constant visitor to the Rossetti's house. To Rossetti Swinburne was his 'little Northumbrian friend', an affectionate reference to Swinburne's small stature—a mere five foot four. Whatever Swinburne lacked in height he made up for in poetic talent. However, with the burden of such great talent came the unveiling of a dark side that was to cause him pain and would, at times, threaten his very existence with all manner of self-inflicted pains through drink, drugs and sado-machoism.

In 1860 Swinburne published two verse dramas; The Queen Mother and Rosamond but it would not be until 1865 that Swinburne would achieve literary success with Atalanta in Calydon.

In 1861, Swinburne visited Menton on the French Riviera to recover from the effects of yet another period of excess use of alcohol, staying at the Villa Laurenti. From Menton, Swinburne then travelled on to Italy, where he journeyed widely.

After Elizabeth Rossetti's death from suicide in 1862, he and Rossetti moved to Tudor House at 16 Cheyne Walk in Chelsea. The stories that survive from his year with Rossetti are typical Swinburne. In one, Rossetti once had to tell him to keep down the noise — he and a boyfriend had been sliding naked down the bannisters and disturbing Rossetti's painting. He took a sardonic delight in what the critic and biographer, Cecil Lang, calls "Algernonic exaggeration": When people began to talk scathingly about his homosexuality and other sexual proclivities, he circulated a story that he had engaged in pederasty and bestiality with a monkey — and then eaten it. How many of the stories were true and how many invented is unclear. Oscar Wilde called him "a braggart in matters of vice, who had done everything he could to convince his fellow citizens of his homosexuality and bestiality without being in the slightest degree a homosexual or a bestialiser."

In December 1862, Swinburne accompanied Scott and his guests on a trip to Tynemouth. Scott writes in his memoirs that, as they walked by the sea, Swinburne declaimed the as yet unpublished 'Hymn to

Proserpine' and 'Laus Veneris' in his lilting intonation, while the waves 'were running the whole length of the long level sands towards Cullercoats and sounding like far-off acclamations'.

Swinburne possessed a curious combination of frail health and strength. He was small and slightly built, but an excellent swimmer and the first to climb Culver Cliff on the Isle of Wight. He had an extremely excitable disposition: people who met him described him as a "demoniac boy" who would go skipping about the room declaiming poetry at the top of his voice. In this as in many things, moderation was not the standard for him. Excess was. Once or twice he had fits, thought to be epileptic, in public; but he made this condition much worse by drinking past excess to unconsciousness. More than once he was delivered to the door in the small of the night, dead drunk. Throughout the 1860s and '70s he rode an alcoholic cycle of dissolution, collapse, drying out at home in the country, then returning to London where he would begin the cycle all over again.

His mania for masochism, particularly flagellation, most probably started in early childhood at Eton and was encouraged by his later friendships with Richard Monckton Milnes (one of Tennyson's fellow Apostles), who introduced him to the works of the Marquis de Sade, and Richard Burton, the Victorian explorer and adventurer. Swinburne was an alcoholic and algolagniac (a desire for sexual gratification through inflicting pain on oneself or others; sadomasochism). He found life difficult, unfulfilling but still his poetic talents pushed to the fore.

Although Swinburne continued to publish some works in periodicals in 1865 he was granted recognition by both public and critics with Atalanta in Calydon written in the style of a classical Greek tragedy.

There followed "Laus Veneris" and Poems and Ballads (1866), with their sexually charged passages, absolutely decadent for polite Victorian society, which were attacked all the more violently as a result. The poems written in homage of Sappho of Lesbos such as "Anactoria" and "Sapphics" were especially savaged. The volume also contained poems such as "The Leper," "Laus Veneris," and "St Dorothy" which evoke both Swinburne's and a general Victorian fascination with the Middle Ages, and are explicitly mediaeval in style, tone and construction. With its publication came instant notoriety. He was now identified with indecent and decadent themes and the precept of art for art's sake.

Swinburne's meeting in 1867 with his long-time hero Mazzini, the Italian patriot living in England in exile, was the beginning of a poetical journey that now became more serious and more engaged with serious thought, initially leading to the political poems in the volume Songs Before Sunrise.

Also in 1867 he was introduced to Adah Isaacs Menken, the American actress, poet and circus rider, whose main fame seemed to be riding naked on a horse (in fact she wore tight nude coloured clothing) for her performance in the melodrama Mazeppa (itself based on a poem by Lord Byron). Although they had a short affair Adah's quote implies that Swinburne was not ready for a relationship that did not involve some self-sabotage; "I can't make him understand that biting's no use."

In 1879, with Swinburne nearly dead from alcoholism and dissolution, his legal advisor Theodore Watts-Dunton took him in, and was gradually successful in getting him to adapt to a healthier lifestyle. Swinburne lived the rest of his life at Watts-Dunton's house. He saw less and less of his old bohemian friends, who thought him a prisoner at The Pines, but his growing deafness also accounts for some of his decreased sociability. By now Swinburne was 42, and was moving from a young man of rebelliousness to a figure of social respectability. It was said of Watts-Dunton that he saved the man and killed the poet.

It is clear that Swinburne had an addictive personality, and clearly incapable of moderation in his pursuit of any chosen vices. This, of course, would both nourish and perhaps sabotage his poetic career. His poetry follows the somewhat clichéd pattern of early flourish and later decline; indeed some of the fresher pieces in the second and third series of Poems and Ballads (published in 1878 and 1889) were actually written during his days at Oxford. Nevertheless, his last collection, A Channel Passage, has some beautiful poems, including "The Lake of Gaube."

He is best remembered as the supreme technician in metre, with a versatility which exceeds even Tennyson's, but which lacks a corresponding emotional range. His obsessions are not widely enough shared; and if he cannot shock us by the strangeness of his desires nor the shrillness of his anti-theistical exclamations, often what remains is not enough to fully engage with the audience.

Swinburne is considered a poet of the decadent school, although he perhaps professed to more vice than he actually indulged in to advertise his deviance. Common gossip of the time reported that he also had a deep crush on the explorer Sir Richard Francis Burton, despite the fact that Swinburne himself abhorred travel. Fact and fiction are easily absorbed by the other so are difficult to untangle even now.

Many critics consider his mastery of vocabulary, rhyme and metre impressive, although he has also been criticised for his florid style and word choices that only fit the rhyme scheme rather than contributing to the meaning of the piece. A. E. Housman, although a critic, had great praise for his rhyming ability: to Swinburne the sonnet was child's play: the task of providing four rhymes was not hard enough, and he wrote long poems in which each stanza required eight or ten rhymes, and wrote them so that he never seemed to be saying anything for the rhyme's sake.

Throughout his career Swinburne published literary criticism of great worth. His deep knowledge of world literatures contributed to a critical style rich in quotation, allusion, and comparison. He is particularly noted for discerning studies of Elizabethan dramatists and of many English and French poets and novelists. As well he was a noted essayist and wrote two novels.

Swinburne was nominated for the Nobel Prize in Literature every year from 1903 to 1907 and then again in 1909.

H.P. Lovecraft, the master of the dark side and a decent poet himself, considered Swinburne "the only real poet in either England or America after the death of Mr. Edgar Allan Poe."

Swinburne was also responsible for devising a poetic form called the roundel, a variation of the French Rondeau form. In 1883 he published A Century of Roundels with several of the roundels dedicated to Dante's sister, the poet Christina Georgina Rossetti. Swinburne wrote to Edward Burne-Jones in 1883: "I have got a tiny new book of songs or songlets, in one form and all manner of metres ... just coming out, of which Miss Rossetti has accepted the dedication. I hope you and Georgie [his wife Georgiana] will find something to like among a hundred poems of nine lines each, twenty-four of which are about babies or small children".

Opinions of the Roundel poems move between those who find them captivating and brilliant, to others who find them merely clever and contrived. One of them, A Baby's Death, was set to music by the English composer Sir Edward Elgar as the song "Roundel: The little eyes that never knew Light".

After the first Poems and Ballads, Swinburne's later poetry was devoted more to philosophy and politics, including the unification of Italy, particularly in the volume Songs before Sunrise. He did not stop writing love poetry entirely, indeed it was only in 1882 that his great epic-length poem, Tristram of Lyonesse, was published, its contents lyrical rather than shocking. His versification, and especially his rhyming technique, remain of high quality to the end.

Algernon Charles Swinburne died of influenza, at the Pines in London on April 10th, 1909 at the age of 72. He was buried at St. Boniface Church, Bonchurch on the Isle of Wight.

Algernon Charles Swinburne – A Concise Bibliography

Verse Drama
The Queen Mother (1860)
Rosamond (1860)
Chastelard (1865)
Bothwell (1874)
Mary Stuart (1881)
Marino Faliero (1885)
Locrine (1887)
The Sisters (1892)
Rosamund, Queen of the Lombards (1899)

Poetry
Atalanta in Calydon (1865)*
Poems and Ballads (1866)
Songs Before Sunrise (1871)
Songs of Two Nations (1875)
Erechtheus (1876)*
Poems and Ballads, Second Series (1878)
Songs of the Springtides (1880)
Studies in Song (1880)
The Heptalogia, or the Seven against Sense. A Cap with Seven Bells (1880)
Tristram of Lyonesse (1882)
A Dark Month & Other Poems
A Century of Roundels (1883)
A Midsummer Holiday and Other Poems (1884)
Poems and Ballads, Third Series (1889)
Astrophel and Other Poems (1894)
The Tale of Balen (1896)
A Channel Passage and Other Poems (1904)

*Although formally tragedies, Atlanta in Calydon and Erechtheus are traditionally included with his poetry.

Criticism
William Blake: A Critical Essay (1868, new edition 1906)

Under the Microscope (1872)
George Chapman: A Critical Essay (1875)
Essays and Studies (1875)
A Note on Charlotte Brontë (1877)
A Study of Shakespeare (1880)
A Study of Victor Hugo (1886)
A Study of Ben Johnson (1889)
Studies in Prose and Poetry (1894)
The Age of Shakespeare (1908)
Shakespeare (1909)

Major Collections

The Poems of Algernon Charles Swinburne, 6 vols. 1904.
The Tragedies of Algernon Charles Swinburne, 5 vols. 1905.
The Complete Works of Algernon Charles Swinburne, 20 vols. Bonchurch Edition. 1925-7.
The Swinburne Letters, 6 vols. 1959-62.